Peter Blitchington

The
Christian Woman's Search
for Self-Esteem

The Christian Woman's Search for Self-Esteem

by

W. Peter Blitchington

Thomas Nelson Publishers
Nashville

Published in Nashville, Tennessee, by Thomas Nelson, Inc., Publishers and distributed in Canada by Lawson Falle, Ltd., Cambridge, Ontario.

Printed in the United States of America.

Unless otherwise indicated, all Scripture quotations are taken from the King James Version of the Bible.

Scripture quotations marked TLB are from *The Living Bible* (Wheaton, Ill.: Tyndale House Publishers, 1975) and are used by permission.

Library of Congress Cataloging in Publication Data

Blitchington, W. Peter.
  The Christian woman's search for
self-esteem.

  Includes bibliographical references.
  1. Women—Conduct of life.   2.   Self-respect.
I. Title.
BJ1610.B55   248.8′43   81-18963
ISBN 0-8407-5797-2   AACR2

Contents

One

Self-Esteem:
Is More Always Better?

Jean had finally been asked out by that boy in her algebra class. Since the class began, she'd been hoping he would notice her. Then, after months of inattentiveness, he had finally asked her out. It had been a lovely evening, she thought. But why hadn't he asked her out again? Maybe it was those long painful silences on the way to the restaurant. Or the inane remarks she had blurted out periodically. She looked at herself in the mirror and breathed a long sigh. No, she thought, the obvious reason is that I'm not very attractive.

It had started out innocently enough. At first Irene's therapist had given her a good-bye hug when she left his office—just an affectionate gesture that she needed at the time. She had come to him because of severe postpartum depression after the birth of her first child. In the beginning, his attentions had comforted her, made her feel good. She felt a surge of excitement when he gave her a quick "hello" kiss. Then it had proceeded to deep, passionate kisses. Now she feels used and degraded. She is seeing another therapist. And she frequently thinks of suicide.

Bernice dreams often about her high school years, especially the night she was chosen prom queen. She remem-

bers her strapless net gown and the way the high school band played when she received her crown. Then she danced with the most handsome boy in the school while all the less popular kids watched in admiration. Those times seem quite far removed from the present. Her many suitors then seem much more interesting now than her husband and her three children. The children cry and make demands, and she feels like pulling out her hair. Her husband comes home weary, wanting peace and quiet, but Bernice wants to go out. She spends her money on the latest shades of eye shadow and the newest lipstick, even though her dresser is already covered with makeup. But she's never satisfied with her looks. Her life seemed more meaningful years ago than it does now.

Dottie has had ten boy friends in the last three months. None of the relationships was very satisfying. None was able to make her feel good about herself. A strikingly beautiful woman, Dottie has little trouble attracting men. But they all seem intent on only one thing. She soaks up their meaningless flattery like a thirsty sponge. Her many boy friends give her no more pleasure nor comfort than did her alcoholic father and her detached mother. Something is missing in all her human relationships. She feels only emptiness inside.

All these case studies involve a common element: self-esteem. More specifically, each involves the experience of low self-esteem. One person feels unattractive and socially incompetent; another feels used. One longs for an earlier time when she was happy and free from responsibilities, while another craves a deep, meaningful commitment in the present.

Self-esteem has become a hot topic for psychologists. We write about it, tell how to achieve it, and no doubt, seek it for ourselves. The desire to feel good about ourselves—to be loved, respected, highly esteemed, and appreciated—is indeed universal.

When I review my own life I'm not aware of a deliberate pursuit of self-esteem. But I can remember in detail things that made me feel good about myself and things that made me feel bad about myself. And of the two, I remember the latter with graphic clarity.

When I recall my growing-up years, I remember experiences that no doubt affected my self-esteem. I think about the relatives with the sharp tongues. A somewhat insensitive family, they had acquired a badgering, teasing manner. And they were very good at it; they seemed to poke fun at the very weakness or insecurity I hoped nobody would mention.

I can still recall some of the "descriptive" remarks they made about me. I suppose their opinions continue to influence my self-concept today. They surely made an impression on me when I was a child.

My experiences during adolescence made an even deeper impression upon me. We're all made vulnerable by the changes puberty creates. Our attractiveness to the opposite sex and our standing among those of our own sex are critical issues. We crave popularity and the esteem of our peer groups, and this craving makes our self-esteem highly unstable.

Adolescence was a particularly stressful period for me because I belonged to that most unfortunate group of handicapped teens called "the late-maturing males." I remember being fairly well adjusted socially until I reached puberty; then all of a sudden many of my friends took off and left me. During the next ten years or so I was just trying to catch up—never mind getting ahead!

The problem of late development was made worse by the fact that I attended a very rough high school. During my first week as a freshman, I walked out of my woodshop class into the crowded hall. I passed directly in front of someone, catching only a glimpse of him out of the corner of my eye. He was a foot taller than I was (as was most of the student population). All of a sudden, he jammed his knee into the side of my thigh so hard that I could not walk for several minutes. I stood in the middle of the hall, grimacing in pain, while everyone walked around me on their way to classes.

These are the sort of images that stand out when I think about early adolescence. I did eventually catch up with, and even physically surpass, most of my high school peers. But I still remember those years of hostile pecking orders. I don't know exactly where I was in the pecking hierarchy, but it wasn't anywhere close to the top!

I don't suppose I've ever had what might be called high self-esteem. My current level of self-esteem would probably be considered "mild" or "average." From time to time it drops a bit, but it rarely rises to great heights.

But is the absence of high self-esteem a bad thing? Verse after verse of Scripture suggests we are not to think more highly of ourselves than we ought.

As I will suggest later, perhaps the best thing to avoid is thinking of self at all. I've been happiest when I've become so wrapped up in an issue, a task, or a goal bigger than myself that my sense of self was lost for a time. Maybe this issue of self-esteem is not as black-and-white as we've been led to believe.

Many psychologists assert that people with high self-esteem are much better adjusted than people with low self-esteem. High self-esteem is important, they say, because it is a much more pleasurable experience than low self-esteem. In other words, "If it feels good, it must *be* good."

However, after studying in some depth the literature on self-esteem, and after evaluating my own experiences, I've come to question some of the common assumptions about self-esteem, particularly the one about the connection between high self-esteem and healthy personality. Therefore, before dealing with some of the specific issues that affect Christian women's self-esteem, I'd like to share some of the observations I've made about self-esteem in general.

Self-Esteem and Healthy Personality

Most of us think we know what healthy personality traits are. At one time I thought I knew—but that was before my counseling experiences. As a psychologist, I used to think human personalities could be divided into two groups: the good and the bad, the healthy and the unhealthy. The bad personalities are anxious, neurotic, introverted, and exhibit low self-esteem. The good personalities are the exact opposite: relaxed, stable, outgoing, and display high self-esteem. You can tell how healthy a person's personality is by simply summing up all his traits and subtracting the "bad" ones from the "good." Whatever is left over indicates how healthy his personality is.

To a certain extent, I suppose this idea is correct. But my readings and experiences have led me to question many of my former assumptions about healthy personality in general and about self-esteem in particular.

Like most psychologists, I was trained by people who focus upon "pathological" rather than "normal" personalities. These mentors classified people into categories labelled "normal," "neurotic," and "psychotic." And the impression was given that one could not have both healthy and unhealthy personality traits at the same time.

What first led me to question this hard-and-fast rule was my experience with psychological tests. My first teaching assignment as a beginning professor was to train graduate psychology students in the art of administering and interpreting psychological tests. The students were required to give several batteries of tests to different people and to bring the results into class, at which time I would interpret the test results. This provided the students with practical experience in the art of test interpretation. But it also provided me with a glimpse into the personalities of "normal" people, since most of the students naturally chose to test friends and neighbors.

I was surprised to find that these people had some of the same weaknesses and characteristics that I had been led to believe only occurred among unhealthy persons. In fact, some of them had quite severe personality weaknesses and yet were still functioning adequately in their day-to-day living. Practically every person, even those who were rated "outstanding," had both obvious strengths and pronounced weaknesses.

At first, this experience shook my faith in the tests. But after looking more deeply into this whole issue of the nature of human personality, I concluded that the tests were accurate. What needed revision was my conception of a healthy personality.

Of course, some personalities are healthier, in general, than others. Severe pathologies such as schizophrenia and psychopathy can in no way be called normal. But the question of what is a healthy personality or a healthy trait is not as clear as it might seem at first glance. Let's look at a few examples.

You'd hardly think there could be any advantages in having a nervous breakdown. And yet, psychiatrist Frederick Flach believes many people become much stronger and more stable after going through such an experience.[1] In fact, he speculates that a nervous breakdown may be a crucial prerequisite to later growth—sometimes you have to break down in order to build up.

A friend of mine went through this building-up process. "I don't believe you have to 'hit the bottom' before you can begin climbing," Ivan said, "but in my case that was so. Only after my hospitalization was I able to come to grips with my needs and accept therapy. Before the breakdown, I could pretend that I was only tired or tense. Afterwards . . . well, there was no use pretending any more."

Other supposedly unhealthy experiences and traits have also been found to have certain compensating advantages. Depression, for example, has been associated with creativity. People who experience periodic depression tend to be more creative than those who don't. Perhaps it depends upon how you handle depression. When Lisa suffered depression after her serious illness and a death in the family, her body was so tired she could hardly function. Her arms and legs were like lead. Yet Lisa determined not to dissolve into self-pity and endless days of soap operas. She had no energy to cook or sew or to do more than basic housecleaning, but she could read. And read she did. She studied everything she could find on a particular subject. Then, after a year of study—still fighting, or rather living with, depression—she began writing a novel, incorporating the elements she'd learned from her reading. The book sold ten thousand copies and is in its second printing. In a sense, this has been very therapeutic for her.

Studies of schizophrenia have yielded similar results. One investigation in Scandinavia found that highly gifted people have more schizophrenic relatives than average people. In fact, behavior geneticists now believe that the gene that carries schizophrenia can be beneficial. If you inherit only one such gene, you'll probably be more creative than most people. The negative effects of schizophrenia will show up only if you inherit a double dose of the gene.

Schoolteacher Faye Evans made Jona's mother feel happier about her somewhat moody, young daughter. "She's so creative, and I understand her. She has that artist's temperament." Faye referred to Jona's tender feelings and her tendency to cry.

Philosophers have long noted that highly gifted people often tend to be more unstable than the average person. But recently that observation has received scientific support. Psychologist Frank Barron reported an interesting study on creativity and personality style in his book *Creative Person and Creative Process.*

A group of highly creative, successful writers and a group of average, less-successful writers were given a test that measures the degree to which a person possesses pathological personality traits. The researchers found that the highly successful writers scored higher on practically all of the pathological traits than the average writers. They were more sensitive, more high-strung, more depressed, and less energetic. *But they also were more self-accepting,* an extremely important trait.[2]

Alan and James, brothers, both had a high interest in

science. They tested high in both scientific aptitude and I.Q., but when they finished college, a difference became obvious.

When Alan tried something—a microbiology experiment, for example—and it proved his basic assumption wrong, he couldn't handle it. He broadly complained, lost sleep, and basically let the failure ruin him. This pattern carried through in everything he did. He didn't even take justifiable pride in his successes, because he figured they were lucky accidents. He couldn't accept his strengths, let alone his weaknesses.

After college he floated from one job to another. "No, I'd never be able to teach . . . No, the position at the pharmaceutical company didn't work out . . . No, that company just didn't understand my abilities. . . ." Today Alan drifts from one job to the next, unable to accept himself or manifest faith in his abilities.

On the other hand, James accepted failure with a philosophical "happens to the best of us," and studied to discover what went wrong. He didn't have a know-it-all attitude, but he always assumed that if he took enough time to study a problem, he could solve it. He failed more times than Alan, because he tried more new ideas.

"Honest pride is better than hypocritical humility," he'd say with a laugh to his friends when an experiment he tried succeeded. After college he did graduate work in zoology. He taught on the college level for a few years before going into paleontology, his first love. Now, with a Ph.D., he is part of a research team and is, in his words, "having a ball."

James was able to accept himself, and so he grew.

I don't want to carry this issue of healthy personality to extremes. But I do want to emphasize that people can't always be evaluated on the basis of "healthy" versus "unhealthy" traits. In fact, what they themselves consider to be bad qualities may not necessarily be so. Sometimes those traits that appear to be the worst liabilities are at the same time the person's greatest assets. Psychologist Zygmunt Piotrowski observes: "What may be a character weakness with fatal consequences under some conditions or in one person may turn into an asset in another individual and in different circumstances."[3]

How Much Is Enough?

What does all this have to do with self-esteem? The answer is simple: *By itself, self-esteem is not necessarily good or bad.* Whether a person has high or low self-esteem cannot by itself answer the question, "How well-adjusted is this individual?" Many other factors must be considered.

I realize that this statement flies in the face of much popular writing. Even some Christian writers have fallen into the trap of using self-esteem as *the* major goal of both childrearing and counseling endeavors. We must have an awareness of our value as children of God, but the central purpose of Christianity is not to elevate self-esteem; it is to redeem sinners. And the person with high self-esteem may be no better off in the areas that really count (such as personal salvation) than the person with low self-esteem. In fact, he may be in worse shape.

Before you dismiss all this as nonsense, consider some findings psychologists have made in studies dealing with self-esteem. Probably the best single work in this area was done by sociologists Edward Wells and Gerald Marwell. Their book, entitled *Self-Esteem: Its Conceptualization and Measurement,*[4] provides a thorough description and evaluation of all the major studies that have been done on self-esteem, along with all the common tests that are used to measure self-esteem.

Wells and Marwell begin their analysis by pointing out that actual research on self-esteem often conflicts with what some psychologists have theorized about self-esteem. For example, as mentioned earlier, many psychologists have asserted that people with high self-esteem are better adjusted than those with low self-esteem. But Wells and Marwell found that research didn't always confirm this assertion. Here's a brief summary of their findings:

1. Persons with high self-esteem are more ambitious, competitive, and self-confident than persons with low self-esteem. They are also more ruthless and egocentric. They maintain a high level of self-esteem by denying any unpleasant facts about themselves.

You've known people like that. They tune out any message that says *they* might be at fault or be less than perfect. Their confidence is so unshakable that they wouldn't think of apologizing or admitting error.

2. Persons with low self-esteem are more anxious and emotional than persons with high self-esteem. They are also more likely to admit their faults and are more open to change.

You've known people like that, too. In high school, Kristen drove her friends crazy by continually saying, "I'm sorry."

"Don't be sorry!" they'd cry. "There's nothing to be sorry about!"

Because of Kristen's low self-esteem, or maybe in spite of it, she made a special effort to dress stylishly, in good taste. After two years of college, she married a young man who was an only child. They stayed together six years or so, with Kristen working for an advertising agency and Brad losing one job after another. Brad's irresponsibility was a large factor in their breakup.

Divorced, Kristen decided to take nurses' training. She remained active in her church and blossomed with the new responsibilities of earning her nursing license. A few years later she married an older man—a father image, perhaps— but they are happy. She once put a note in the "Personal Lines" section of the newspaper. "To Theodore, who has made me happier than I ever thought possible." Her ability to genuinely appreciate her loved ones stands out like sunshine on a winter day.

Wells and Marwell conclude that, overall, the results of studies relating self-esteem to adjustment tend to "favor the high self-esteem position, but the evidence is not at all clear-cut." To confuse matters even more, one study found that neither persons with high or low self-esteem were well adjusted. The high self-esteem persons were "narcissistic," and the low self-esteem persons were self-rejecting. This study indicated that *it's best to have a moderate level of self-esteem.* Too much or too little can be bad.

Two factors may help explain why the research on self-esteem is not more consistent. In the first place, as mentioned earlier, people can't be evaluated on the basis of only one attribute. Even if persons with high self-esteem were always better adjusted than persons with low self-esteem, we don't evaluate ourselves only according to the sometimes vague standard of "adjustment."

In some areas, the person with low self-esteem might be better off than the one with high self-esteem. The anxious person with low self-confidence may be more open to the changes induced by the Holy Spirit. Christian evangelists from the time of Paul have preached that you must develop a sense of self-distrust before you can be led by the Spirit. Paul wrote in Romans 12:3 that the Christian was "not to think of himself more highly than he ought to think." Some theologians have speculated that self-dependence is the basis of all other sins. For if we depend only on God, and not on ourselves, we will be kept from all types of sin.

Is it possible that the person with low self-esteem finds it easier to depend on God than the person with high self-esteem? Can high self-esteem sometimes become a barrier, preventing us from calling upon God and impelling us to rely upon ourselves?

A second reason for the inconsistency of self-esteem research is that several different types of self-esteem seem to exist. In the next chapter we will look at seven sources of self-esteem.

Two

What Is Self-Esteem?
Where Does It Come From?

Self-esteem is a difficult attribute to understand, let alone measure. For the individual, self-esteem is a very concrete experience; but for the professional, it's an abstraction. And it is extremely difficult to measure an abstract trait in human beings, who are composites of many different attributes.

But on another level, self-esteem is hard to measure because it is influenced by so many different factors. In fact, I suspect that at least seven types or sources of self-esteem exist. The list is not meant to be inclusive.

1. Self-Esteem That Depends on Love

The most important source of self-esteem is the experience of having been loved by our parents. In the early years of childhood, one's parents represent God. We gain our most profound understanding of His love through the love we receive from them—His representatives.

If we aren't loved by our parents, the chances are good that we will be unable to love others unreservedly. Toby has always resented that statement. "What am I supposed to do—be a hermit because my dad abused me and my mom didn't stop him?" Yet married now, with children of his own, Toby realizes that he never learned to love. At nearly forty years of age, his concept of God has grown so that now he views God as totally interested in every aspect of his life. This is a comfort to him, but he still has trouble accepting love from his wife and giving it to his kids.

We learn to commit ourselves to others, in part, by experiencing our parents' commitment to us. Feral children, human beings who were deserted by their parents and raised by animals, illustrate this principle. Only a few have ever been studied by doctors, but in every case the pattern is the same: these young people are never able to form deep attachments to others. The bonds of commitment are slack, never having been strengthened through parental love in the early years.

People who were unloved by their parents suffer in other ways as well. They often grow up with a craving for love, which makes them susceptible to the influence of anyone willing to give them even superficial doses of love. Some homosexuals prey upon young boys who are neglected by their parents. Pornographers and pimps wait in bus stops, looking for young children who have run away from home. Often they are able to lead these children into prostitution with a few kind words and a candy bar.

One of the sadder stories I've read was that of an attractive young woman who lived in California several years ago. As reported by a newspaper, she came from a well-respected, middle-class family and was good-looking and popular with her peers. But her self-centered parents were so wrapped up in their own interests that they neglected to give their daughter the security that comes from being deeply loved. She craved attention from powerful men and became involved with several underworld figures. She provided them with sexual favors, and they stimulated her with alternating doses of attention and sadistic abuse. One night they apparently got tired of her, and she was brutally murdered.

So the feeling of worth that comes from having been loved by both parents is the most important type of self-esteem. Without it, it is difficult for people to reach their full potential as adults. Often they either suffer from an unfulfilled craving for love or they become hostile and prone to violence, often making others suffer along with them. This doesn't mean that everyone who was unloved as a child is irrevocably and hopelessly sentenced to a life of low self-esteem. I know two men who were both raised in bad home situations, unloved and uncared for by their fathers. One indeed has a hard time accepting and giving love, but the other is one of the most loving, giving men I've ever known. He's very good with his children.

I don't know if the self-esteem that comes from parental love is the sort the tests measure, but family love is certainly the most important source of healthy self-esteem.

2. Self-Esteem That Depends on Living Up to Standards

In what has become a classic study on the development of self-esteem, psychologist Stanley Coopersmith found that favorable self-attitudes are found in children whose parents set high standards for them and who love and accept them.[1] Apparently, children value themselves according to how well they perform tasks and how well they meet ethical and religious standards.

Terry's mother considered eating between meals a cardinal sin, ranking up there with lying or disrespect to one's parents. If a neighbor offered her an apple between meals, Terry would say, "No, thank you. But I'll take it home and eat it with dinner." This would make her mother obviously proud, boosting Terry's ego. Terry adopted her mother's attitude toward eating between meals and later tried to instill it in her daughters as well.

One Sunday morning the family visited a new church, and the Sunday school leader offered the children apples and cookies so they wouldn't be hungry during church. Terry's daughters ate with the rest of the children. Terry was angry and crushed. Her identity as a good child and a good mother received a painful blow, and she had a hard time dealing with it. This may seem silly, but a good deal of Terry's self-esteem depended on instilling that standard in her children.

Development of self-esteem by performing tasks does not

have to be a negative thing. Children who are given specific jobs around the house soon take a pride in their work and in being part of the family team. Parents who are too busy to train their children in this way are doing them a great disservice.

A great sense of self-approval results from our ability to live up to high standards. We feel competent and effective when we meet those standards, and we are kept from debilitating feelings of guilt.

But there should be a warning here for Christians. Deriving self-esteem from living up to standards can lead to a doctrine of works, which can have two results. People who fail to live up to the standards they have set for themselves (or in some cases, standards others have set for them) may feel they have failed miserably and be unable to accept forgiveness. On the other hand, those who feel they do live up to the standards set for them are in danger of developing spiritual pride. Jesus said, "Blessed are the poor in spirit" (Matt. 5:3). He was referring to those who recognize their need for and dependence upon God, not those who have little spiritual reserves. The opposite of "poor in spirit" is "proud in spirit." Jesus was no doubt thinking about the Pharisees, who took great pride in their piety and righteousness.

We Christians can't let our self-esteem hinge upon how righteous and good we are. Certainly, living a sanctified life protects us from guilt and condemnation. And surely a life of sin, in which we fall far short of our standards and God's, fills us with remorse, self-condemnation, and despair. But that doesn't mean we earn self-esteem through our righteous lives. We live righteously because God Himself gives us the power to do so.

3. Self-Esteem That Depends on Comparisons With Others

This is the poorest of all the sources of self-esteem, but it is one of the most common. All too often we fall into the trap of comparing ourselves with others and feeling good (or bad) about ourselves to the extent that we are more attractive, more gifted, wealthier, or in a higher position or social class than others.

This orientation begins early in life. We can see it among children, who argue such issues as "my dog's better than your dog." During adolescence the issues shift to such things as beauty, masculinity or femininity, and the best car or clothes. But if in adulthood we get pulled into the race to "keep up with the Joneses," our self-esteem rises or falls according to how successfully we stay on top.

This is a bad pattern to fall into. For one thing, it is ultimately self-defeating, because there will always be someone prettier, richer, more talented, or more sociable. For another, it encourages materialism and makes us look to other people as our standard rather than to Christ. I don't know who comes out the worst—those on top or those on bottom. The ones who come out on the short end often become restless and dissatisfied; those who come out on top tend toward arrogance and materialism. It's hard for either to be receptive to the Holy Spirit.

When I began teaching in a university setting, my wife and I became acquainted with another couple who had fallen deeply into the competitive trap. This couple had formed a clique with several other young couples, and there was quite a struggle among them to see who could stay on top. Each would make snide remarks about the other couple's possessions; none seemed content or satisfied. It might have been amusing had it not been so tragic.

4. Self-Esteem That Depends on Acceptance by Others

This source of self-esteem is closely related to both the first and third sources listed above. The need to be accepted by a peer group is particularly strong during adolescence. Young people often form tight groups and try to protect those groups from the threat of outsiders.

One young woman told me the following story:

I was very popular during my early elementary school years. I got along well with both boys and girls. Then in the sixth grade my parents put me in an exclusive private school. The pupils there had very status-oriented parents. The girls formed a clique, and at the head of it was an attractive, outgoing girl. It was amazing to watch how effectively she worked. Every week some student got ostracized, and the leader always decided who it was. The other girls picked up on it and stopped speaking to her; they wouldn't even invite her to parties. For some reason the leader disliked me and made me the frequent target of her disapproval. I think the two years I spent in that school did more to rob me of my self-confidence than all the other embarrassments I've ever had put together.

Shelly had a social problem with a different twist. She'd attended a small country school from grades one through five. For the past three years she had been the butt of ridicule and teasing by two older girls in her room. She had spent hours in tears, dreaming about how life would be different someday.

Then her parents moved to another state, and Shelly entered a large school that was as different from her first school as night is from day. She gradually formed a corps of close friends. But one girl, Marcie, was not included.

"I could like Marcie," Shelly confided to her mother. "I feel sorry for her because the other kids tease her. But I can't afford to like her. I've never had friends before, and if I show that I like her the other kids won't like me."

We marvel that we never seem to learn.

Several years ago, sociologist Charles Horton Cooley came up with an interesting theory about how we come to view ourselves. He theorized that we see ourselves through the eyes of others, by watching how they treat us and how they react to us. The earliest and most important "mirror" is our parents. That is why it is so important that we as parents affirm our children rather than criticize them. Later, friends and peers take over. Finally, the society as a whole plays an important role.

Together, these forces have a strong impact on the way we feel about ourselves. Rejecting, disapproving parents can often set a pattern that determines how peers react. The rejected child may be overeager or resentful around his friends, thus incurring even further rejection. People can end up in a powerful self-perpetuating cycle. This is why a counselor prefers to work with the parents as well as the child when a child has personality problems. Often, one or both parents have contributed to it.

5. Self-Esteem That Depends on Accomplishment

Surprisingly, this is one of the least important and most fleeting sources of self-esteem. But lost and lonely people grasp at this to make them feel better about themselves. Sixth-grade Monica had never felt accepted at school, and she also had problems with her parents. She began setting her alarm for five in the morning to get up and study, determined to make straight A's and to finish her books months before her classmates. Missing a quiz question reduced her to tears. Her normal desire for good grades became a compulsion as she sought self-esteem through her accomplishments.

If a person has been loved and accepted by his parents, achieving some measure of success can often enhance self-esteem. But many famous people have taken their own lives because of an unmet craving for love and a fear that they are unlovable.

Christians should be especially careful not to feel superior about God-given talents. Intelligence, energy, a pleasing personality, beauty, and wealth are all endowments from God. As such, they are to be dedicated to His service in some way, not used to wield power or influence over other people. I recently talked to a man who used to feel contempt for people who couldn't "carry their own burdens," or who needed other people. Then he fell victim to depression, and his attitudes changed. He experienced the extreme fatigue and mental weariness of depression and became very thankful for friends who stayed with him and who are helping him weather this crisis.

6. Self-Esteem That Depends on Temperament

Temperament is one of the most frequently overlooked contributors to self-esteem. Studies indicate that some people have high self-esteem simply because they are biologically predisposed toward feelings of self-confidence and self-worth. Those of us who don't live on an emotional high might find this personality enjoyable, disgusting, or simply confusing. One young woman confided in me: "I've always envied my friend Cindy. Nothing gets her down or discourages her. Nothing can shake her faith in herself. Even when she was a little girl, she met strangers with complete self-assurance, even boldness. She's made of stronger stuff than I am."

Others have low self-esteem because of an innate predisposition toward hypersensitivity and anxiety. They must learn to judge their lives by reality, not by how they feel.

Clinical psychologist Theodore Millon wrote an excellent textbook entitled *Modern Psychopathology*.[2] In it he described two different types of pathological personalities. The "aggressive personality" is bold, arrogant, domineering, pugnacious, and hateful. The "avoidant personality" is shy, withdrawn, insecure, and fearful. Ironically, both personality types can spring from the same sort of background—parents who are overbearing, cruel, rejecting, and hostile. Aggressive children, with bold, insensitive, "choleric" temperaments, so thwart and upset their parents that the children come to see themselves as powerful "forces to be dealt with." But avoidant children, with sensitive, anxious, "melancholy" temperaments, are completely intimidated and cowed by their parents. The same situation that lowers the self-esteem of one child can raise the self-esteem of another.

Some people have such strong inborn tendencies toward optimism that they may even distort defeats and embarrassments in order to make them look like victories. I remember Muhammed Ali's response to his first defeat, at the hands of heavyweight champion Joe Frazier. The day after he was beaten, Ali was humble and apologetic. Two days later he was offering excuses for his defeat. Within a week, Ali was talking as if he actually had won the fight. He had recovered all of his old arrogance and braggadocio.

People with this type of temperament almost always have very high self-esteem because they have an innate resistance to any suggestion of failure, defeat, or embarrassment. In contrast, some people have low self-esteem because of an inborn tendency to magnify defeats and humiliations. People with this temperament will interpret even harmless statements as insults. Tabby was so sensitive she would scrutinize compliments for hidden meanings. If a friend said to her, "That's an attractive hat you're wearing," she would analyze each word to discover its "real" meaning. Usually she convinced herself that her friend actually meant to demean her. This is exactly the opposite procedure that someone with a temperament like Muhammed Ali's would initiate.

7. Self-Esteem That Depends On Society's Estimation

One final source of self-esteem results from society's approval or disapproval of who you are or what you do. The collective opinion that makes up what we call society can easily affect the way you think about yourself. Society has definite reactions to one's skin color, job, social class, wealth, appearance, and other factors. This tendency is so strong that Christ specifically instructed that we avoid treating some people better than others.

Janis is overweight. She dies a little inside every time someone tells a "fat" joke or when strangers point at her on the street. She's tried all the diets, and finally one is helping her lose weight. But at eight hundred calories a day, she's always hungry.

Doris, who is one hundred pounds overweight and has battled obesity all her life, has turned to a different solution. She recently had her stomach stapled so that all it will hold is one fourth of a cup at a time. There are unpleasant side effects, but in a society that demands thinness Doris could never feel good about herself and be overweight.

Women who see their most important role to be caring for children and family are not given much encouragement from our society. In fact, they often face open disapproval and hostility. I will cover this issue in other chapters, so I won't go into detail now.

Societal approval as a source of self-esteem is much less potent than is parental love. But it still has an influence. People long to know that they are needed and that what they do is important.

These are the major sources of self-esteem. There may be others. My point is that we can't really speak effectively about self-esteem unless we designate the type of self-esteem we mean. Low self-esteem in some of these areas may be extremely painful; in other areas, it may be irrelevant. We all need to feel loved and valued; we all need to feel important to someone else. On the other hand, having very mediocre accomplishments is only as important as you wish to make it.

Madeline Jones' two daughters are complete opposites. Karen is happy and accepts herself, while Lucy is always discouraged and convinced that she's no good. Both girls are talented in music. Lucy is a good gymnast, and Karen enjoys art. But no matter what Lucy accomplishes, she thinks she should have done better.

The more we look at this issue of self-esteem, the more complicated it becomes. All too often, psychologists have assumed that self-esteem depends on only one main source and that the more self-esteem you have, the better. It's not that simple.

To make matters even more complicated, psychologists disagree about exactly *what self-esteem is* just as much as they disagree about *where self-esteem comes from.* Before covering the factors that affect the self-esteem of women, I'd like to give you a brief description of how self-esteem is usually defined.

What Is Self-Esteem?

I recently had an interesting discussion with another Christian psychologist about the role of self-esteem in the Christian experience. Upon learning that I was writing a book about the self-esteem of Christian women, he asserted that "we have to get our terms right. When we talk about Christians, we're referring to the experience of self-worth, not self-esteem. Self-esteem is how you feel when you rise above other people or triumph over them. It is another term for egotism and therefore has no relevance for Christians. Self-worth, on the other hand, is what you feel when you know that God loves you, has died for you, and has given you a special personality and function that no one else has."

This discussion illustrates the point I made before: Even professionals do not agree on a definition of self-esteem. And yet we must be able to offer at least a general definition of this experience or attribute if we hope to be able to communicate clearly.

Self-esteem usually is defined by psychologists in one of three ways. These three definitions should enable us to understand the *process* or *experience* of self-esteem; they should give us an idea of what self-esteem feels like and looks like on tests and in our everyday behavior.

1. *Self-esteem is a global attitude.* According to this definition, self-esteem is one overall experience. It may have many different sources, but it is still one attitude. Tests that use this approach simply ask you to check a number of traits or attributes. The more positive ones you attribute to yourself, the higher your self-esteem. Sometimes self-esteem is defined as the number of positive traits minus the number of negative traits. Your level of self-esteem is what's left over.

If self-esteem is compared to a lake, this definition would say that your level of self-esteem depends upon how full the lake is. A full lake is better than a half-full lake. It doesn't matter where the water comes from, as long as there is a lot of it.

Thus an attractive Christian woman who grew up in a loving home will have higher self-esteem than an unattractive Christian woman who grew up, in a loving home, according to this definition. You simply find the sum of the positive attributes. A more sophisticated approach would involve "weighting" the different attributes. But this definition still sees self-esteem as *one* attitude that flows from the number of positive qualities you possess.

2. *Self-esteem is an evaluation of your attributes and experiences.* According to this definition, self-esteem depends not so much upon the *number* of positive qualities you have as upon your *evaluation* of those qualities. Tests that use this approach also ask you to check the traits that apply to you. But in addition, they require you to go back through the list and indicate how the presence or absence of those attributes makes you *feel* about yourself.

This method would see self-esteem as a lake that has several rivers running into it. The important thing is not how full the lake is but what type of rivers it is fed by. A small lake fed by two "good" (important) rivers might be better than a large lake fed by two "bad" (unimportant) rivers.

This method has several advantages over the first. For one thing, it recognizes that self-esteem changes as the different *sources* of self-esteem change. Thus it allows for different types of self-esteem. Also, it recognizes that some sources of self-esteem may be more important than others. Self-esteem will change qualitatively and quantitatively, with changes in the sources of self-esteem. Finally, it recognizes that finding the sum of a person's attributes is not enough. You must also ask him what he *thinks* about those attributes.

According to this definition, two different women with the same attributes may differ in self-esteem as a result of their different estimations of those attributes. Jean is a plain-looking woman with two attractive, successful Christian children. Her husband has achieved a modest amount of success in the world and is now retired, on pension. Jean still works at a fairly well-paying job. Joanne is also a plain-looking woman with two successful, attractive Christian children and a retired husband who has been modestly successful in his work. Joanne has just retired from a fairly well-paying job.

Despite their similar experiences and attributes, Jean and Joanne have widely differing levels of self-esteem. Jean is an ambitious woman who wanted her husband to rise to the top, not just pay the bills on time. She also values physical attractiveness and lavish displays of wealth, neither of which she possesses. Thus, she is extremely dissatisfied and unhappy with herself.

Joanne, on the other hand, has never been bothered by the fact that she is not Mrs. America married to a corporate president. Material wealth and external beauty are not high on her list of priorities. She wanted her children to grow up to be strong Christians, as they have. Joanne is much happier and feels much better about herself than Jean.

3. *Self-esteem is a discrepancy between our real self and our ideal self.* The third and final definition sees self-esteem as a product of what we would *like* to be minus what we *are.* This method is usually calculated by asking a person to (a) check all the attributes he would like to have, and then to (b) check all the attributes he possesses *now.* His self-esteem is the difference between (a) and (b). The larger the gap, the lower the self-esteem.

In terms of the lake analogy, your level of self-esteem would depend not only upon how full your lake *is,* but also upon how full you would *like* it to be. The person with a large lake would not be well off if he thought he should have an even larger one.

This method is somewhat similar to the evaluation approach. But it still sees self-esteem as one *global* experience. And it doesn't allow for the different sources or types of self-esteem or for qualitative as well as quantitive differences in self-esteem.

It does, however, recognize the importance of the standards we set for ourselves and the degree to which we meet or fall short of those standards.

These are the three most popular definitions of self-esteem. Each contributes something to our knowledge of this attribute and explains how self-esteem is measured. But of the three, I think the "evaluation" definition is the strongest. Self-esteem does not depend solely upon what we have or what we are, but also upon how we evaluate our traits, our experiences, and our personalities.

This definition allows us to assess the various factors that influence the way we feel about ourselves. It gives us some hope and some control over our self-esteem; we can change our evaluations even if we can't change our past experiences or current problems.

What This Book Can Do for You

Women in general, and Christian women in particular, seem to face some unique threats to self-esteem. Several years ago, Dr. James Dobson circulated questionnaires to Christian women in order to identify their major problem areas. He found low self-esteem at the top of the list.

I believe these self-esteem problems result in large part from the way women have been encouraged to evaluate themselves. The messages women are hearing about themselves are unflattering. Chapter 3 identifies those hostile messages and suggests ways to counteract their influence. The first step in waging an effective battle is to know one's enemies, and these cultural messages and forces *are* enemies.

Women show a great diversity in personality styles and traits. Chapter 4 attempts to encourage an appreciation of varying personality styles by giving special attention to four types that have often been disparaged.

Self-esteem is also strongly affected by marital roles and relationships. In a constantly changing social system, our family roles and responsibilities are also changing rapidly. Adjusting to these changes and to new ideologies has been a major task for women and men. Chapter 5 deals with the effects of marriage and sex role patterns upon women's happiness and self-esteem. Chapter 6 describes six basic types of marital relationships, with special attention given to the strengths and weaknesses of each type and the effects of each one on the wife's self-esteem.

The ways in which men and women differ from one another can also engender self-esteem problems among women, especially since male attributes have been overvalued and female attributes undervalued. But sex differences shouldn't frighten us. God purposely created us male and female, and when we understand that purpose and our unique sexual natures we not only will come to understand femininity but we will cherish and respect it as well.

Various aspects of the feminine nature will be covered in several different chapters. But two dimensions of femininity are discussed in detail: woman's sexual nature and her energy level. My readings have convinced me that both men and women misunderstand the feminine sexual response and often experience conflict as a result of that misunderstanding. My own research has shown me that many women suffer energy crises that affect their self-esteem, due to the many demands placed upon them and because of the differences between male and female energy levels. Chapters 7 and 8 offer suggestions for understanding and dealing with these differences in sexual drive and energy level.

One of the central differences between men and women is that women's lives are more sharply divided into stages. This is especially true of married women. Beginning at adolescence, when menstruation abruptly signals the onset of puberty, women are faced with more clearcut changes in their lives then men. Males go through puberty, of course, but the changes are more gradual.

For most women, there follows school, marriage, career interrupted by motherhood, departure of the children, perhaps followed by career again. Men usually have a much easier time reconciling their different roles—husband, father, worker—than do women, who are more likely to be pulled in opposite directions by their different roles. Added to this, menopause comes along to bring another sharp change in women's lives. Finally, the loss of a spouse in the later years is a more frequent problem for women than for men. Men die earlier, leaving women with another abrupt role: widowhood. In order to preserve healthy self-esteem, women must devote more attention to the transition between, and the integration of, their different roles.

Chapter 9 covers the major stages and changes in a woman's life. I write with the assumption that what happens at one stage affects one's self-esteem in consequent stages, and with the desire to help readers make the best possible adjustment at each stage of their lives.

Finally, the last chapter offers several specific suggestions for dealing with low self-esteem. These suggestions will help make it possible to implement some of the material covered in the previous chapters and will provide fresh material and procedures not covered elsewhere in the book.

One final thought: I believe anyone can profit from this book—married or single, male or female. Although it is aimed primarily toward women, and slanted toward married women, it contains much about self-esteem in general.

Three

Social Forces
Hostile to Christian Women

"It's so hard to be a Christian today."

Strangely enough, I hear that refrain often in one form or another—even from committed Christians.

No doubt it is an accurate statement. Many temptations exist today that weren't around even twenty years ago. But the assault upon Christian principles goes beyond simple temptations to self-indulgence. Today, Christianity has to compete with alternate ideologies, and it must resist hostile challenges to its most important tenets.

Our grandparents and their ancestors didn't face the same challenges that confront Christians today. This isn't to say they had it easier than we do. On the contrary, in many ways their lives were more difficult. But they lived in a time when society accepted certain universal absolutes. Christianity and Christian principles were respected; rarely were our forefathers driven to confusion by competing ideologies.

Today that situation has changed. Christian principles and the people who uphold them have been buffeted by one assault after another. In the early part of this century, Darwinism and Freudianism led the charge. Now the assault comes from a wide array of pop psychologists, sociologists, "open marriage" advocates, and avant-garde pseudointellectuals. Their influence, combined with many recent social changes, has not only cast doubt upon the principle of self-denying love; it has also elevated selfishness and narcissism to a position of ideological respectability.

Charlotte is quite noticeably caught in the dilemma over standards and values. Reared in a very strict Christian home, she developed a traditional set of values. Yet she wants to be flexible and open to changes in society as a whole.

I remember an interesting conversation my wife and I had with Charlotte, her husband, and another couple over dinner one winter night about two years ago. The conversation started off on the topic of homosexuality. Charlotte said that "homosexuals have been given a raw deal; we should give their lifestyle as much respect as we give heterosexuals."

When the conversation moved to the virtues of chastity, Charlotte spoke about the drawbacks of her strict upbringing. She saw little virtue in her premarital continence, she said, and if she had it to do over again she would not restrain herself. She felt sure that her own two daughters will probably "live with boy friends before they are married."

My wife and I were surprised by Charlotte's frank rejection of traditional Christian values. But Charlotte became even more surprised and confused by a string of events that happened to her about a year after our dinner conversation.

Her first shock came when one of her closest friends called, in tears, to say that her husband had run off with another man. Her friend was devastated and had to spend several months under psychiatric care to get herself together.

Soon after recovering from that shock, Charlotte's sister moved in with her boy friend. But this live-in arrangement didn't work out as ideally in reality as it had in fantasy.

A third confusing blow came when another of Charlotte's friends, a divorced mother, moved in with her boy friend. I remember something Charlotte said soon after she learned of this arrangement. Sitting on our sofa while talking to my wife, she gazed off into space and said, "I wonder how she'll ever be able to teach her daughter any moral standards.''

Charlotte's dilemma is common to many Christians today. We want to be flexible and ''keep up with the times,'' but so often the times themselves are out of step with Christian principles. In fact, many of the current popular philosophies and ideologies are downright hostile to Christian virtues and to the men and women who adhere to those virtues. Yet when the once forbidden is embraced by everyone from entertainers to popular thinkers to our best friends, it is no wonder that we begin to question and reexamine our values.

These new ideologies and social pressures affect all Christians, young and old, male and female. But they have created special difficulties for both single and married Christian women. Psychotherapist Richard Hagen describes the effects of changing cultural messages upon the self-esteem of many married women.

> Many women are now coming for counseling because they can't escape the current campaign telling them that the only fulfilled woman is the professional woman and that having and raising babies is definitely out. These women are trying to conform, but deep inside they want to have and raise babies.[1]

The new cultural messages that downgrade family roles and responsibilities lower the self-esteem of many women who have devoted themselves to their families. At the same time, single women feel pressured by the new morality to have sexual relationships outside of marriage, often with a variety of partners, and teen-age girls guard the fact of their virginity as a ''dirty little secret.''

I recently read *Solo Flight,* an interesting book about the single Christian.[2] It confirmed observations I had made about the single lifestyle: that sexual pressures are tremendous and that many single Christians are on the defensive because of these pressures.

''I'm tired of trying to defend my decision for premarital

chastity,'' college student Robin declares. ''It's almost tempting to pretend I've given up sex as a penance for something, or that I'm above such earthy pleasures because I'm so bright.''

She sighs. ''Isn't it ridiculous? It's like the guys try to get you in bed the first thing, and when they discover you won't, they dump you for someone who will.'' Her dark eyes flash fire. ''That kind of girl isn't considered 'loose' any more. Just normal.''

I'd like to briefly describe several of the most nagging social movements and pressures that are hostile to Christian virtues. Some affect both men and women. Others are hostile mainly to the Christian woman. All run counter to biblical principles.

The Fractured Family System

Depression has reached epidemic proportions among women in this country. Estimates suggest that anywhere from two to six times more women than men suffer from depression. A woman's greater susceptibility to depression begins in adolescence and continues throughout her lifetime.

These startling statistics were recently reported by science writer Maggie Scarf in her best-selling book *Unfinished Business*.[3] She decided to investigate the problem of female depression after her best friend, a gifted and attractive woman, tried to kill herself. After that completely unexpected episode, Scarf began an investigation into female depression that took her into some of the country's leading psychiatric institutions. She conducted scores of interviews with women in different walks of life. Her interviews bore out the statistics: Women are depressed in alarming numbers.

Her stories make fascinating reading, in part because we so easily recognize the women she interviews. We see them in our friends and acquaintances: mothers whose husbands have left them; women living with their boy friends, craving a more tangible evidence of commitment yet fearing they'll be left if they demand it; women with noteworthy achievements who admit feelings of worthlessness and depression.

Searching for a cause for this epidemic of female depression, Scarf observed that women are torn between their own desire to form "bonds of attachment" with parents, children, husbands, or lovers, and the cultural pressure and personal desire to form an independent identity of their own. According to Scarf, these attachments or bonds are of crucial importance for both working women and homemakers, both single and married women.

A book entitled *Gender and Disordered Behavior* studies sex differences in rates of mental illness.[4] One chapter is devoted to the topic of depression among men and women. It presents all the technical studies and statistics on depression that have been gathered, not only in this country but in many other nations and cultures as well.

The epidemic of female depression is occurring in other countries besides the United States. In fact, *women are more depressed than men in practically every industrialized nation.* So strikingly consistent are these statistics that one wonders if female depression is an inevitable outgrowth of industrialization.

Before we conclude that the high depression rate among women is inevitable, consider an interesting study that was reported in *Gender and Disordered Behavior*. Researcher Walter Gove found a community in France where women were actually depressed *less often* than men. Apparently, this is one of the few (perhaps the only) industrialized societies where such an observation has been made. This community has a strong family system. The divorce rate is low, family relations are warm and positive, and the people feel a sense of belonging and mutual commitment.

We can't escape the fact that our values, happiness, and self-esteem are closely related to our family system. Whatever affects our society affects all of us. And the quality of our family system definitely affects our society.

Probably the best sociological work on the relationship between type of family and type of civilization was done by Harvard sociologist Carle Zimmerman. In 1947, he published an amazing book entitled *Family and Civilization,* in which he showed the common pattern of the family systems of all great civilizations.[5]

In the early years, all civilizations have a primitive extended family system, with relatives living with or near one another. Then, in their most productive years, great societies have a strong nuclear family (called the domestic family). Husbands, wives, and children are committed to one another; the divorce rate is low; a good balance between individualism and family responsibilities gives the society both creative initiative and moral and social strength. The final stage comes when the family system falls apart. Husbands and wives lose sight of their commitment to one another and to their children, and the society begins to weaken and disintegrate until it is conquered by a more powerful nation (with a stronger family system).

This pattern is so predictable that Professor Zimmerman has listed ten signs that *always* accompany the weakened family system.

- a skyrocketing divorce rate
- a plummeting birth rate
- a growing disrespect for parents and parenthood
- an obsession with the weaknesses and failures of ancient heroes, accompanied by a loss of patriotism
- an emphasis upon companionate (or open) marriage as the solution to the weakened family system
- a refusal by many people to maintain family responsibilities while everyone else "goes free"
- the hostility pseudointellectuals have for the family spreads to the common man; then *no one* cares
- a rampant increase in adultery
- juvenile delinquency and rebelliousness toward authority
- an acceptance of perversions of all kinds, especially homosexuality

Sound familiar?
The weakening family system affects everyone, but it

seems to have its most negative impact upon family-oriented women. Dr. Zimmerman reports that Roman intellectuals derisively considered devoted married women with children "domestic prostitutes"; husbands divorced their wives and took up with childless prostitutes.

Divorced men are more likely to remarry than divorced women. And when they do remarry, it is usually to women who are much younger than their first wives. This typically produces the sad phenomenon of thousands of middle-aged women growing old without husbands. No doubt this creates among women strong insecurities about family life.

We Christians must lead the way in promoting strong families. The sense of well-being and self-esteem women need depend upon it. Perhaps more importantly, the freedom to live openly as Christians is jeopardized as the God-ordained institutions of marriage and family are discarded in favor of perverse, hedonistic lifestyles.

Sexual Freedom

The breakdown in the family system accompanies an increase in sexual freedom and a pressure to participate in nonmarital sexual experiences. Those who don't wish to participate are often given unflattering labels that suggest they are out of step with the times. Many "experts" tell us that greater sexual freedom will make us more creative, less neurotic, happier, and more fulfilled.

Typical of the assault upon Christian sexual standards is a new book by John Money entitled *Love and Love Sickness*.[6] Dr. Money, a well-respected medical psychologist, is a staunch opponent of the Christian church—an organization he feels is responsible for much unhappiness due to its "repressive" standards. He likens "sexual oppression" in America with political repression in the Soviet Union. Our society, he charges, is guilty of being a "sexual dictatorship," preventing us from enjoying the free expression of our sexuality. And the main culprit behind this dictatorship, he feels, is the church.

This attitude is surprisingly common among popular writers today, who claim that the old puritan standards have caused us much mental anguish and that monogamy is a barrier to growth. Sexual freedom would not only make us less uptight and less neurotic, they say; it also would enable men and women to trust one another and develop friendships, both sexual and nonsexual, more easily.

If anything, the sexual revolution has had the opposite effect. It's been especially hard on women, who are less able to separate sex from emotional commitment (a noble characteristic, I might add). The new doctrine of sexual freedom has engendered much hostility between men and women, for it has given some men a weapon with which to pressure reluctant women into bed. It has introduced a strong opportunity for sexual exploitation into male-female relationships. Women who participate don't know (or want to find out) if they are loved for themselves or for the short-term gratification they provide.

Lisa will never forget her first sexual experience. "I was a college freshman and under much pressure because I'd never 'done it.' Jeff seemed a nice enough guy—he didn't grab at me on the first date or anything like that. When he asked me to spend Sunday afternoon in his dorm room, I knew what he expected and I decided, why not? What's so precious about my virginity? No man cares about it nowadays anyway."

She twisted a wheat-colored strand of hair through her fingers, uneasy but obviously needing to tell someone. "We sat on his bed and kissed, then we lay on his bed and . . . made love." Tears filled her eyes. "Then he leaned over and flipped on the TV."

"It was so casual to him . . . so *nothing*. I felt like he'd wiped his feet on me!"

Her voice dropped. "Tell the girls that they may not think their virginity is so great, but it's nothing to be given away to someone who doesn't even care."

Unlike Lisa, Deb didn't want to share the whole story. She's fifteen and in the ninth grade. "I never expected Dale to marry me, but afterwards he wouldn't even speak to me in the hall. I was used," she said, echoing a common refrain in this sexually free society.

On a recent Phil Donahue show, a writer described her newest book on different types of men. Many women called in to complain about their relationships with the men in their lives. Much of the questioning revealed concern with their lovers' motives for maintaining the relationships. I couldn't help but notice that these questions came almost exclusively from women who were living with men outside of marriage. Their self-esteem was threatened by the possibility that they were being exploited.

The lowering of sexual standards actually encourages people to exploit one another, making people the means to an end. Several recent court cases have been won by women who were taken advantage of by their male therapists. Also, many working women complain of "sexual harassment" by their bosses, who demand favors in exchange for benefits. So common is the problem of sexual exploitation that psychologist George Albee, a former president of the American Psychological Association, in a recent professional article charged that the sexual freedom movement is "undermining the work ethic."[7]

Of course, sexual freedom is directly opposed to the teaching of Christ, who designated marriage as the only acceptable context for sexual intercourse. Sexual freedom puts pressures on young men and women, erodes marital relationships, and leads people to believe that happiness can be found in self-gratification.

Christian sexual standards actually make it easier, rather than more difficult, for single men and women to share genuine friendship without fear of exploitation. High moral standards nullify ulterior motives and allow single women to have greater confidence that they're being appreciated as persons rather than as sex objects.

Preference for the Masculine

One of the most pervasive and subtle assaults upon feminine self-esteem has been the tendency to prefer masculine values and attributes at the expense of feminine ones. This is especially true in American culture.

Psychologist Judith Bardwick recently published an interesting book entitled *In Transition*. In it she reviews several studies that indicate that both men and women in America have so come to value masculine traits and goals that we characteristically overlook and even denigrate feminine attributes and experiences.

In one study college students in Norway, Sweden, Denmark, Finland, England, and the United States were asked the question, "What would you like to be like?" In every country, the students agreed on the traits they considered masculine and feminine. But only in the United States did both men *and* women identify the masculine qualities as the ideal. The other students had much more positive attitudes toward feminine traits. Bardwick summarizes the effects of such attitudes as follows:

> To a grave extent, women . . . do not esteem those of their characteristics and contributions they perceive as feminine. It is not plausible to imagine that one can develop a sense of one's worth at the same time that one holds oneself in contempt. The disdainful regard for homemaking and mothering is based not just on the citation of boredom, tedium, and no pay. That withering judgment is also the expression of sexism.[8]

She goes on to explain that this preference for the masculine has been an unfortunate result of the women's movement. Some extremists have even demanded that biology be used to eradicate sex difference. In her best-selling book, *Women and Madness,* psychologist Phyllis Chesler urges that science be used to "release women from biological reproduction" so they can more easily compete in the masculine world.[9] Another feminist, Shulamith Firestone, joins the Central Committee of the Chinese Communist Party in calling the new artificial birth technology "a happy day for women." Fewer working days will be lost, it seems, because of pregnancy and childbirth.

These are extreme views, obviously. But they still reflect the common cultural opinion that men's lives and attributes are fascinating, while those of women are dull and unimportant. These attitudes cannot be pleasing to our Creator, who created us male and female for a purpose. It takes both feminine and masculine characteristics to make up the "image of God." Our culture must learn to appreciate the gifts that are uniquely feminine if women are to experience self-worth and esteem themselves realistically.

Four

Turning Weaknesses
Into Strengths

In this chapter we will look closely at four personality types. Each personality style described has both strengths and weaknesses, and personality growth is achieved, obviously, by developing the strengths and controlling the weaknesses.

If there is any one area in which psychology should be knowledgeable, it is the area of personality. The field of psychology is almost synonymous with the term "personality." Much work has been done in this area, but a large part of it is useless, and some of it is downright misleading.

Part of the blame for this failure of psychology to provide practical knowledge about personality has to be borne by Freudian psychoanalytic theory. This theory has much breadth and depth, but its fixation upon sex, its various Oedipus and Electra complexes, its obsession with neuroses and disturbances instead of with the healthy side of personality, and its preference for complicated symbolic interpretations all too often make learning difficult and impractical for the layman who wants to understand his own personality. Despite these serious limitations, psychoanalytic theory has been one of the dominating forces in the area of personality theory.

Personality theory has also been dominated by behaviorism. In its purest form, behaviorism asserts that personality is the result of learning. We are all empty slates at birth, and the rewards and punishments we receive determine the personality traits we have. Therefore, we never have any real choices; we are what we are because of our parents, our school, our society, and all the other controlling agents in our lives.

Certainly, we are partly products of our environments. But there is much more to us than that. This idea of behavioristic determinism robs human beings of their free will—a gift from God. It makes us passive recipients, rather than active initiators. It rejects the traits and predispositions we acquired through our genes. And finally, it really doesn't help us understand our own personalities. The many forces in our environments that mold and shape us are so varied and so complex that we simply can't put them together into a coherent explanation of ourselves. I find that behaviorism, and learning theory in general, simply doesn't provide people with what I call the "aha" experience—that moment or mental process of self-revelation that is needed if we are to understand ourselves.

Two Myths About Personality

Several other false notions have contributed to a misconception of personality.

1. *There is one best personality.* Most of the personality theories I've seen both in professional literature and in the popular press suffer from a serious limitation: They fail to convey adequately the great amount of diversity found among healthy people. As mentioned earlier, variation is one of God's greatest gifts to mankind. What a boring world it would be if all plants and animals looked alike! And how dull and drab it would be if all human personalities were similar.

Although we all have the same moral code to live by, we are not bound by the same standard or ideal in our personality development. Each of us has different talents, attributes, and styles of acting and expressing ourselves. Most of us enjoy finding our own best styles rather than mimicking the styles of others.

Of course, some personality styles are preferred above others. The "in" personality style in our culture is extroverted, tolerant and flexible, spontaneous, and egocentric. In ages past, the ideal personality was introverted, task-oriented, and less flexible. If your personality style is not the preferred one, your task may be to ignore cultural pressures and accept yourself as you are.

This is one reason it is hard to evaluate whether a single attribute is good or bad. How can we say whether one specific personality trait helps or hinders unless we can see the whole personality? Recall again the statement by psychologist Zygmunt Piotrowski: "What may be a character weakness with fatal consequences under some conditions or in one person, may turn into an asset in another individual and in different circumstances."[1]

What we need is a detailed analysis of personality that assumes people are innately different and that what may work for one person may not work for another. This approach would also assume that every personality trait or style has both positive and negative aspects.

For example, Harvey is a quiet, bland man who might seem boring and unattractive. But his steady, easygoing nature is just the right style in his nerve-wracking, pressure-filled job. And his personality is just the right complement to Susan, his vivacious, spontaneous, and excitable spouse. Susan puts excitement into his life and draws him out socially, while his easygoing personality balances her "highs."

2. *All personality is learned; nothing is inherited.* This myth was started back in the 1920s, when John Watson, the father of behaviorism, made his famous statement:

> Give me a dozen healthy infants, well-formed, and my own specified world to bring them up in and I'll guarantee to take any one at random and train him to become any type of specialist I might select.

Watson and B. F. Skinner are considered extremely ardent behaviorists. It's interesting to watch the reactions of diehard behaviorists when you mention that heredity plays a role in personality or intelligence. When I was a graduate student in psychology, one of the professors was lecturing on the role of heredity in personality. Several Skinnerian behaviorist students turned over desks and loudly protested his material. "We've got the gospel according to Skinner," said one, "and that's all we need."

Some psychologists recognize that heredity plays a role in personality development, but they fear that people will use heredity as an excuse for not changing. Instead of trying to overcome a hot temper or a weakness for liquor, some people might lament, "It's my nature. I'm just like that."

Certainly, heredity shouldn't be used to defend the status quo. Christians have access to a power that can help them control even the most strongly inherited characteristics. But the great danger of overlooking heredity is that we fail to help people understand themselves and develop their own unique gifts and attributes. More than that, we might cause people to lose self-esteem.

For example, Heidi is quiet and shy, preferring books and long walks to parties or even being with a group of her peers. Then she reads a bit of self-help advice: "You can be anything you want to be."

Heidi realizes that the extroverted, outgoing people get the most social rewards, so she decides to be an extrovert.

It's hard to speak to everyone she meets instead of looking away, but she manages that. The small talk comes harder. Her jokes fall flat. She makes an effort to join parties, but in a deep corner of her mind the frivolity bores her. Bright lipstick enhances her smile, but it doesn't reach her eyes.

After trying all the self-improvement advice the book has to offer, Heidi finds she still would rather work in the garden alone or with a close friend than work up a lot of false enthusiasm over people and things she's not interested in. Two months later she gives up in defeat, as shy as ever.

If Heidi really believes the "you-can-become-anything"

philosophy, then after failing to become an extrovert she is likely to feel that something is wrong with herself, that she is an unusually inept person who can't do anything right. By setting up a false premise—that personality is infinitely malleable—some "pop" psychologists give people misleading standards.[2]

These self-improvement "experts" send us off on wild goose chases after personality styles and attributes we don't have much potential for. This causes us to overlook the gifts and potential we do possess, while preventing us from achieving the prerequisite for personality growth and development: self-acceptance. I am not suggesting that you passively accept your every weakness; rather, you should try to accept your general personality style, with the intention of developing and growing within that style and of accepting the roles and functions it thrusts upon you.

Heredity *does* play a strong role in determining our personality styles. According to some of the best research I've seen in the field of personality, the four-temperament theory of Hippocrates has more scientific support behind it than any other theory of personality, including psychoanalytic and behavioristic theories. This four-temperament theory is one of the few explanations of personality that gives people that "aha" experience they need if they are to understand their own personality styles.

Although the four-temperament theory has been around since Hippocrates, it wasn't really investigated scientifically until about forty years ago. Beginning in the early 1940s, British psychologist Hans Eysenck began a series of studies on human personality that eventually established the accuracy of the four-temperament theory.[3] He showed, through hundreds of well-controlled laboratory studies, that two dimensions of personality account for most of the traits found in human beings. The two dimensions are: (1) introversion—extroversion, and (2) high emotional drive—low emotional drive. When you put the two together, the four temperaments emerge as shown below.

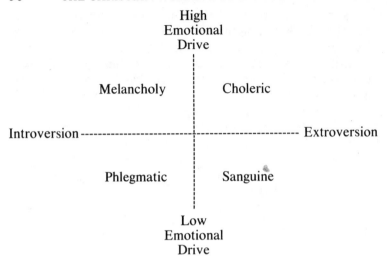

The temperaments that evolve from these two dimensions of personality have the following characteristics:

    Melancholy—anxious, compulsive, moody, depressive, high-strung, sensitive, shy.

    Choleric—driven, impulsive, ruthless, willful, easily bored.

    Sanguine—adaptable, optimistic, flexible, well-adjusted, scatterbrained.

    Phlegmatic—submissive, tolerant, slow, even-tempered, good-natured.

Eysenck further demonstrated that *temperament is mainly under the control of heredity.* It results from inherited features of the brain and body chemistry, although learning no doubt plays a role.

This should not produce a fatalistic, shoulder-shrugging reaction from Christians who don't particularly like their own temperaments. God designed a world in which diversity, variation, and healthy individuality would reign. Each temperament has a gift to offer, a role to fill, and a unique function to perform. The key to personality growth is not to attempt to "become anything you want to" but to develop the uniqueness you've been given, perfecting your strengths and controlling your weaknesses.

The first step in this process is an honest self-evaluation—a detailed look at your own predispositions, strengths, and weaknesses. I believe the four-temperament theory is the best starting place for the woman who wishes to understand her own gifts and attributes.

I would like to describe four personality styles, closely related to the four temperaments, that some "experts" think are undesirable. Actually, each of these styles has both strengths and weaknesses. Perhaps you will see yourself in one of these descriptions.

The Introverted Woman

Introversion is probably one of the most misunderstood personality styles in existence. One book says you can assess how introverted or extroverted you are by your "degree of selfishness." The more introverted you are, the more self-centered and selfish you are. The more extroverted you are, the more you like people and give unselfishly.

An introverted person who believed this rubbish would no doubt experience a drop in self-esteem and would long to acquire a different temperament. The first step in personality growth—self-acceptance—would be impaired. And her gifts and strengths would be neglected.

Actually, whether you're introverted or extroverted depends upon how certain parts of your brain are constructed.[4] The same part of the brain that keeps you alert and attentive also makes you introverted or extroverted. Here are some of the characteristics often found among introverts and extroverts. Keep in mind, as you read these descriptions, that whenever we deal with human personalities we're talking about predispositions or tendencies, not hard-and-fast traits.

1. *Mental attitude.* Extroverts tend to be more optimistic, happy-go-lucky, and cheerful than introverts. This tendency has both positive and negative features. On one

hand, this optimistic mental attitude makes extroverts more self-assured and confident than introverts. They approach new tasks with an air of confidence, which often helps them overcome procrastinating tendencies. They make new friends more easily; they optimistically expect acceptance while introverts anticipate rejection. Their positive mental attitude makes them feel more energetic and enthusiastic. We all admire their open, spontaneous friendliness.

But the introvert's more negative mental set also has good features, within reason. His pessimism often makes him plan better and try harder. The extrovert's optimism can lead to overconfidence; the introvert knows he must try hard if he wishes to succeed. Sometimes an optimistic, happy-go-lucky attitude makes extroverts irresponsible. Introverts, on the other hand, are more conscientious and meticulous. Studies indicate that they are more persistent and efficient workers than extroverts. They have fewer accidents, change jobs less frequently, and work harder.

This conscientiousness and pessimism can, of course, be carried too far. Some people are so pessimistic that they are afraid to try anything new. They avoid anticipated failure by refusing to act at all. They can become over-conscientious to the point of carrying the weight of the world on their shoulders. This can cause feelings of despair and depression much like those Elijah (an introvert, no doubt) experienced after his victory over Ahab on Mount Carmel.

The introverted woman's goal should be to develop her conscientiousness without becoming so serious-minded that she makes herself a stick-in-the-mud. Angela decided she could turn her inborn pessimism into an attribute by anticipating problems and then planning ahead to meet them. She refused to expect failure in everything she tried, even though she had a natural tendency to do so.

Angela found that calling upon God for help was a great source of comfort and strength when she was faced with a new situation where she just "knew" she'd fail. While planning and preparing for the problems inherent in her new experiences, she also memorized certain Bible texts that gave her courage. Philippians 4:13 became one of her favorites: "I can do all things through Christ which strengtheneth me."

2. *Moral development.* Introverts have a stronger conscience, a more sensitive response to guilt, and a greater concern for morality than extroverts. In part, this is due to childrearing characteristics. Introverted children are easier to train; they learn rules and standards much more easily than extroverts. Because extroverts are more distractible and happy-go-lucky, it takes much more effort on the part of parents to instill high standards in them. Studies have shown that a disproportionately large percentage of criminals are extroverts, while a greater number of neurotics are introverts.[5] The extroverts are more prone to lawbreaking, the introverts to feeling guilty.

I suspect this difference accounts for the greater tendency of introverts to join churches. In fact, many of the biblical patriarchs and prophets seem to have had tendencies toward introversion. Their sense of morality and conscience made them especially receptive to the leading of the Holy Spirit. However, extroverts are more likely to bubble over with joy about their relationship with Christ and will lead others to Him.

The introverted Christian woman often needs to avoid an overly critical attitude. Mrs. Humphrey's high standards and strict conscience made her somewhat legalistic and harsh on others. While studying the life of Christ, she realized that she should keep her standards high but at the same time cultivate an attitude of compassion and patience toward others. Mrs. Humphrey often felt guilty because she did not reach real or self-imposed standards of right behavior. She had to learn to exercise faith in God and in His promise to forgive sins and shortcomings. She eventually learned to give God her guilt and to accept His peace.

3. *Social relationships.* Almost everyone would agree that the area of social relationships most clearly distinguishes introverts from extroverts. Extroverts are friendlier, more talkative, outgoing, and interested in people while introverts are shy, sensitive, and creative. But the

most important distinction is that extroverts like people and introverts don't—right?

Although this is the popular conception, it's simply not true. No research anywhere suggests that extroverts "like people" more than introverts do. The research does indicate that introverts have fewer friends, but *they often have more intimate, long-lasting relationships with those few friends*. Extroverts, on the other hand, make new friends and drop old friends more easily than introverts. They do not seem to need the deep relationships that introverts need.

But it is true that introverts are more shy, less outgoing, and more detached than extroverts. The reason is not that introverts like people any less, but rather they prefer less stimulation than extroverts. Extroverts are stimulation-seekers. Since other people are stimulating, extroverts seek them out. Introverts, on the other hand, are stimulation-avoiders, preferring peace and quiet. They tend to avoid large gatherings and noisy social events. The reason introverts prefer less stimulation is that their central nervous systems are more sensitive. Too much novelty and activity makes them uncomfortable.

This helps explain the reasons behind the painful experience of shyness. Psychologist Phillip Zimbardo's *Shyness: What it is; what to do about it* sold a million copies, indicating the large number of people who want to overcome that characteristic. Zimbardo offers much helpful advice for shy people, but he fails to emphasize what I consider the most basic lesson: shyness itself has certain positive features that need to be emphasized. As a British psychologist observed more than fifty years ago:

> Shyness is so common, at least in this country, that we tend to accept it as something inborn, as a characteristic part of the charm of youth, and as evidence, when it persists into later years, of a certain fineness of character; it seems even to be a trait, perhaps not wholly to be deplored, in the national temperament.[6]

The writer Isaac Bashevis Singer is even more optimistic about the positive side of shyness (perhaps because many writers are themselves shy). He asserts that:

> I don't think that people should get over being shy. It is a blessing in disguise. The shy person is the opposite of the aggressive person. Shy people are seldom sinners. They allow society to remain in peace.[7]

Zimbardo observes that shyness allows a person to stand back from social relationships and assess people before getting involved with them. A lack of shyness may cause some people to rush into things before they know what they're getting into.

Shyness is generally associated with creativity, high moral judgment, and esthetic talents. Further, a shy person makes a good mate for an outgoing person; the two complement one another.

I will elaborate on these advantages in the next section. However, the important issue is *how you handle your shyness*. Many women are extremely shy and yet quite well-liked and attractive. They are the ones who have learned to accept their shyness and make the most of it. Others allow their shyness to erect barriers that turn people away.

Responsiveness is an important factor in the social effectiveness of the introverted woman. Alice is shy, somewhat withdrawn, tongue-tied, detached, and feels ill at ease in new situations. Yet she has many friends *because she is warm and responsive*. The shy woman who has problems making friends is the one who rarely smiles, who acts defensive and tense when approached, and who gives the impression that she would rather not be bothered. She lets her fear obliterate her more attractive qualities. I know a shy woman who is devoted to her family, has a strong character, and likes people. But her stone-faced appearance turns off people who would like to be her friends. If she would only smile more and respond warmly to people, her shyness would cause fewer social problems.

The Sensitive Woman

Sensitivity occurs more often among introverts than among extroverts and has both advantages and disadvantages. The sensitive woman is often more discerning, esthetic, and perceptive than the insensitive woman. But she is also more timid and inhibited and more prone to depression and listlessness. We all know people who are hurt by imagined slights.

These differences have special meaning for women, who tend to be more sensitive than men, at least in some areas of their lives. For one thing, women are more sensitive to physical pain.[8] We don't know which sex can tolerate the most pain, but we do know that women feel pain more easily. They are also more sensitive to sensation—touch, taste, smell, and sound. Since emotional sensitivity is tied in with physical sensitivity, it follows that on the whole, women are more sensitive to emotional pain and to the needs of others than are men. This emotional sensitivity may account for what we usually call "woman's intuition."

Sensory (or emotional) insensitivity has both positive and negative features. The insensitive person is more resistant to both emotional and physical pain; illnesses and fatigue don't have a strong effect on him. This helps him to be more energetic. He ignores his own pain and trudges ahead, while the sensitive person may magnify his pain and feel overwhelmed by it.

The insensitive personality style is the one that's admired in the popular press. The person who pushes ahead despite pain, working long, hard hours to reach his goals, is the one who gets the applause in our culture. But there's a strong negative side to the insensitive personality style, one that's usually overlooked by the media.

For one thing, the same personality trait that makes him insensitive to his own pain and emotions also makes him insensitive to the needs of others. Insensitive people always make enemies, and all too often their families suffer for lack of attention and concern. Further, this type of person is often insensitive to principles, standards, and rules. Studies have shown, in fact, that the most eminently "successful" people have strong traits of ruthlessness and egotism in their characters. These traits may serve them well in the business world, but they wreak havoc when it comes to Christian service and standards. The insensitive person can rarely be an effective witness for Christ until he learns to handle the negative side of this personality trait.

All too often, the insensitive person ends up with few friends and a shortened life. This was the case with Mr. Steiner. Constantly overlooking the demands of his own body, he eventually wore himself down and ruined his health. His final years were sad, for he had alienated his family and had made many enemies; loneliness and poor health prematurely terminated his life.

The sensitive personality style has some weaknesses, too, although these are too often emphasized to the detriment of the strengths. The sensitive person is more subject to mental stress, depression, and neurosis. The great physician Simmelweiss, a sensitive man, took over the directorship of a large European hospital before doctors knew about such things as infectious bacteria. It seems young women who entered the hospital to have babies were becoming ill and dying at an alarming rate. The doctors who touched and examined the pregnant women were doing so often after performing autopsies on people who had died of various diseases.

After some experiments, Simmelweiss decided that something carried on the hands of the examining doctors was killing these new mothers. As the director, he passed a rule that doctors had to wash their hands with an antiseptic before examining patients. This new requirement almost immediately lowered the death rate among these women. But rather than appreciating the results of this new requirement, the doctors resented having to wash their hands, and they were angry at Simmelweiss for his restrictions. They so harassed and condemned him that this sensitive man eventually had an emotional breakdown and ended up in a mental institution.

The sensitive personality is often an introvert who forms

deep emotional attachments to other people. My wife, Evelyn, once met a shy, aloof, detached woman. This woman—I'll call her Marge—was very hard to talk to, but Evelyn kept trying until she found a topic of mutual interest. Because of Marge's initial aloofness, Evelyn thought nothing would ever come of the conversation. She was amazed when Marge called and invited her to go shopping. Soon a close friendship developed. Marge and her family eventually moved to another state, but she continues to telephone my wife on a regular basis. In a socially mobile nation, people who establish deep commitments are invaluable and irreplaceable.

Finally, sensitive people are very perceptive and discriminating in their judgments. They are aware of subtleties that less sensitive people do not discern. I recently read a biography of Augustus Caesar. In my opinion, he was one of the shrewdest politicans who ever lived. Before he became emperor, Rome was rapidly collapsing. But after his reign, Rome enjoyed its most prosperous era. His clever political insights and ingenious plans for strengthening the family were responsible for Rome's longevity.

In this biography, the author pointed out that Augustus was anything but an imposing figure. He was small, delicate, and not especially vigorous. The biographer also observed that Augustus was a sensitive person, concluding that only a very sensitive mind could have achieved what he did.

If you are a sensitive woman, you have gifts that can be of great value if you cultivate them properly. Your deep commitments and sensitive conscience are valuable attributes, and your keen perceptions and judgments are useful to anyone willing to listen. I believe sensitive people can be more sensitive to the leading of the Holy Spirit than emotionally insensitive people. (The negative side to this trait, however, is the tendency to act in accordance with one's intuition without really making sure the impression is from God.) Though the sensitive personality style is rarely given the praise and applause of bolder, more aggressive styles, it is no less valuable.

The Emotional Woman

The highly emotional personality receives little appreciation from the popular press. According to the messages we get from television and books, the ideal personality is cool, emotionally uninvolved, and even-tempered. Strong emotions are liabilities, according to popular thinking. The highly emotional person has an affliction that must be cured.

The truth is, high emotionality can be either a strength or a weakness, depending upon how it is handled. Properly channeled, strong emotions can be a great source of energy and creativity. When mishandled, however, they can lead to moodiness, nervousness, anxiety, and impulsiveness.

Everyone knows what it feels like to be in a state of high emotion. Just think about how you felt when you gave your first public speech. Your heart raced. Your breathing was rapid and difficult. Your voice quivered. Your knees shook. Your hands perspired. You might have felt like running away. Your body, in fact, was programmed for action.

Emotion is a great energizer. Said William James, father of American psychology, "There is no action without emotion."

Samuel Beck, another well-known psychologist, puts it this way: "Man's intellect is an indispensable resource in his growth. . . . But he can advance no further than his inner force, his total emotional resources . . . can propel him."

Clinical psychologist Zygmunt Piotrowski states the case for emotion even more bluntly: "A person devoid of emotions displays very little activity, either mental or physical." He goes on to say that strong emotions may sometimes cause people to make impulsive decisions, but those same emotions are still the impelling force behind all activities.

If you are a highly emotional person, you may be tense, impatient, high-strung, anxious, or insecure, but when you learn to channel those strong emotions you will become charged by an abundant supply of energy.

In fact, often a person cannot successfully complete a difficult task until his emotions have been sufficiently aroused. Dr. George Crane, who wrote a syndicated column called "The Worry Clinic" for more than twenty years, once described the difficulty he had motivating himself to write the column.

His standard procedure was to set aside one day a week in which to write the six columns. He would arise early on the designated day with every intention of completing the task as quickly as possible. But he couldn't seem to get started. After breakfast he would read the morning paper, stalling as long as possible. Then he would choose six case histories from his files. But instead of getting right to work, he would adjust his typewriter ribbon or oil the type-writer—anything to avoid the difficult task of putting words together into sentences.

There followed some procrastinating rituals, such as drinking a soda, calling his downtown office, and wandering around looking at his professional journals. Soon it would be time to eat lunch.

The longer he would put off writing, the more irritable, emotional, and anxious Dr. Crane would become. One might think Dr. Crane simply wasted the morning. But in actuality, this period of procrastination was necessary to galvanize Dr. Crane's emotional energy into action. Once his emotions had built to a sufficient level, the words would almost erupt onto the paper. Dr. Crane recognized this when he observed that "it is only when my emotional ire reaches the eruptive or volcanic state that I can actually percolate mentally."

So we see that properly channeled emotion can be a source of energy and creativity. However, this doesn't mean the emotional person is not without problems. Highly emotional people do more poorly in jobs that involve pressure and stress than do emotionally stable people. They are more prone to worry. And some studies indicate that highly emotional people are less popular than emotionally low-key people.

One of the tasks of a highly emotional woman is to learn

to handle pressure and stress. Daily prayer sessions, asking God for peace and serenity, are necessary. Learning to "worry" optimistically—using her gifted imagination to envision positive images—is of crucial importance. Reading inspirational literature, such as the Bible, should help channel the emotions into a positive frame of mind. Self-acceptance provides the foundation upon which these actions are built. When the emotional woman realizes God's purposes for her, she will be on the road toward a positive use of her own personality style.

The Submissive Woman

Submissiveness is another personality trait that's been condemned by the popular press. In fact, "submissiveness" has almost become a dirty word lately; few people dare to admit it is part of their personality. Today's popular traits are the polar opposites of submissiveness—independence, assertiveness, aggressiveness. Women in particular are being urged to shed any submissive tendencies they might have.

This thinking completely overlooks the strengths of the submissive personality style. For one thing, the give-and-take of living together at home, at work, and at school requires at least a certain amount of submissive acquiescence. Often the person who is unable to submit, cooperate, and compromise makes a poor worker, and an even poorer mate. I've seen intelligent and capable students drop out of college because they could not submit to the requirements of their teachers. In some cases, this independence served them well in setting up their own businesses. But it usually also cut short their formal education.

Submissiveness is a crucial personality trait in the Christian experience. We are told to be "submissive" (cooperative, yielding, adaptable) to one another (Eph. 5:21). In a sense, this type of submissiveness is a counterpart of humility, meekness, and other Christian virtues. It does not mean an absence of initiative, energy, or independence, but rather a willingness both to accommodate other people's needs and desires and to repudiate our own selfish ambitions and desires when these would lead to strife or cause unnecessary conflict among fellow Christians. One man I know has practically ruined his influence in the church he pastors because of his inability to submit. He makes decisions affecting the entire church without consulting the elders or the church board. He has already lost several longstanding members.

A submissive woman is a perfect complement for an aggressive, decisive spouse. She often serves as a level-headed, down-to-earth balance for her husband's energy and spontaneity, in much the same way that the emotional woman provides the spark in her marriage to a more even-tempered spouse. Without these complementary characteristics, the active husband might become too aggressive and the stable husband might be too dull.

So we see that there are many different personality styles. Each has strengths and weaknesses. No one personality is complete in itself. We all need one another to provide a balance, with one personality providing what another one lacks. Within this context, God's intention is to restore the original strengths to each personality style, control the weaknesses, and let diversity and variety manifest themselves. We should learn to appreciate—not condemn—this diversity, no matter what our culture says.

As you analyze your own personality style, ask yourself, "Is my style a popular one in the eyes of the culture I live in?" If it's not, then the chances are good that you will not appreciate your personality.

The solution to this dilemma is not to try to acquire a new personality style but to develop the strengths of your own style, ignoring the preferences of the culture. Remember, culture is fickle and not always reasonable in its choices. In 1774, Goethe published a book entitled *The Sorrows of Young Werther*. This book advanced the idea that genius was closely connected to madness. The book's genius hero took his own life. Soon after that, madness became popular as a sign of creativity and giftedness. Many young artists adopted eccentric, weird personality traits, and a rash of suicides spead over Europe. People began to act sick because that was what their culture said was desirable.

Our culture today says the Christian life is no longer desirable. Our challenge is to ignore that message.

Five

Marriage, Sex Roles, and Feminine Self-Esteem

With all the intellectuals' attacks, and all the comedians' jokes, marriage would seem to be anything but a source of self-esteem and growth. But the act of marriage itself says that someone loves you enough to commit his life to you. It's the only self-chosen human relationship that is embodied by law and made sacred by religion.

However, marriage is not utopia. Even (or perhaps especially) the best marriages go through continual periods of adjustment. Sally Smith falls head over heels in love with Freddie Jones. She dons a white gown and veil; her father pays two months' salary for the festivities; and Sally and Fred are duly wed.

It's a modern marriage, so Sally works "at least until the babies come," and although they don't write out a formal contract as some couples do today, Fred helps around the house.

After the first few months they don't bother to make up the bed (by mutual agreement), and Fred generally takes out the garbage. Once a week they bustle around and give the place a quick cleaning. Married life isn't so bad after all.

Except that Sally takes forever in the bathroom.

Except for Fred's socks. Sally swears his socks have a life of their own and actually breed and multiply all over the bedroom floor when her back is turned.

Other problems creep up. Sally leaves the towels in the

64

dryer instead of folding them. Fred doesn't like streaking through the house, shivering, hunting a towel after his shower. Once Sally left a clean load of clothes in the washer for two days, and they soured. They'll do that, especially in warm weather. Fred was not very happy about the unique odor of his briefs.

Living with Fred is no bed of roses either, much to Sally's dismay. Mom always told her there is nothing dumber than a man, and Sally is beginning to believe it. The socks, for starters. After a year, he still leaves them where they fall.

And there's another problem. It's silly and too insignificant to mention, but . . . Sally puts a lot of stock in greeting cards, and Fred has yet to buy her one. For their first anniversary they went to a restaurant atop the tallest building in the city. The view was fantastic, and the food was great. Afterwards they made leisurely love, and Sally had never been happier. Except . . . except for that one little thing that rubbed like a pebble hidden in a tennis shoe. Fred had hardly glanced at the anniversary card she'd taken so long to select for him, and *he didn't even buy her one.*

Marriage requires maturity, but how many of us enter marriage with a full bag of that elusive quality?

Little annoyances explode into all-out battles. Biting one's tongue continually is no fun and doesn't even solve most problems. They just pop up again and again.

Many of us resent having our mobility and freedom curbed. Angie loves water skiing, but David can't swim and is not comfortable around water. Jeri went to football games with Kyle before they married, but she never understood what all that running back and forth was about. Now she can't stand the sound of the televised game in the house.

Angie goes water skiing with her friends, while Dave stays home and putters around the yard. She wonders why he's miffed when she returns. Jeri tells Kyle to go ahead to the football games, but begrudges the money he spends on tickets and the time he spends away from her.

Every married couple soon realizes that they have a lot of

adjustments to make. One personality, one ego, one set of strengths and weaknesses must somehow be meshed with another.

Many anti-family philosophers can't understand how people could be subjected to the sort of growth-inducing experiences that marriage requires and still report that they are, in general, happier than single people. Some feel compelled to explain away the satisfaction and happiness of well-adjusted married couples by suggesting they are self-deceived.

The Future of Marriage, by sociologist Jesse Bernard, is a typical product of someone who sneers at traditional married living.[1] In one chapter of this book, she compares the advantages enjoyed by four groups: married men, married women, single men, and single women. This research suggests that men gain more clearly observable benefits from marriage than do women. Men gain in the areas of mental and physical health, social enjoyment, economic productivity, and happiness, while married women have no advantages over single women in any of these areas, except one—happiness. In fact, married women actually score lower than single women in some of those areas.

On the basis of this research, Dr. Bernard is impelled to ask why, "in the face of all the evidence, so many more married than unmarried women report themselves as happy? As, in fact, they do." In other words, Dr. Bernard cannot understand how married women can say they are happier than single women.

I find her explanation for this finding most interesting, although insulting to women. She declares that women are happier when married because they have been socialized (or "deformed," as she puts it) into believing they should be satisfied with marriage. She completely ignores the possibility that marriage can provide genuine sources of pleasure and happiness.

As George Gilder points out in his best-selling book *Sexual Suicide,* this negative attitude toward married living usually comes from people who have grown up in an atmosphere of power, position, and material wealth.[2] These early experiences make it hard to understand how women could enjoy the care and nurturing of children (jobs they associate with "hired help") or how marriage could serve as a source of satisfaction and happiness (when they associate satisfaction with privilege, position, and power). With this sort of orientation, it's no wonder that some privileged people are hostile toward marriage, the traditional female role, and the women who enjoy filling that role.

Of course, traditional marriage and childrearing require attributes that today's world does not especially respect. The disintegrating family system, of which we see daily evidence, may cause us to feel anxious and insecure over the stability of our own marriages. If it could happen to so many, perhaps it could happen to us. So why put one's energy into such a fragile institution? Put it into one's own self-fulfillment instead. Certainly power and position can enhance one's sense of self-worth. (This is especially true in a society that considers power more important than love.)

Happiness is an elusive, evanescent state. But one thing seems certain, judging by all marriage studies that have been conducted: Married people say they've found happiness more often than unmarried people do. This is true for both men and women.

Of course, this does not apply to each and every married couple. Many are miserable, as is obvious from the high divorce rate. And many single people are quite content.

Neither do these statistics say a single person can't have a good self-image. Perhaps their self-image depends on how they view their singleness. Flo and Janice believe God has called them to a life of service that requires them to remain single. Whether or not you agree with their philosophy, the fact is, they are on good terms with themselves and are happy in their work.

Violet Adams has spent thirty years of her life as an elementary school teacher. "People tell me I shouldn't get too attached to my children," she told me, "but I don't think it hurts. I've never had a family, and these kids are my life."

Many a mother of a shy or mischievous youngster has blessed Miss Adams for her outpouring of selfless love on their children. Miss Adams finds her identity in working with other people's children. She wanted children of her own, but her life took her down a different road, and she feels good about herself. She is content.

Judy, on the other hand, has fought a lifelong losing battle with obesity. Naturally thin people can have no understanding of Judy's problem. Nor can they understand why her self-respect is shattered every time she sees some scantily clad skin-and-bones beauty advertising diet cola on TV.

"A woman without a man is like a fish without a bicycle," she told a friend of mine seriously. "Who needs one!"

Judy does. Or rather Judy needs someone whose tenderness and genuine delight with her forty-pound-overweight body make her feel like a woman. Her protests only reveal her deepest desire—her desire for an intimate relationship with a man, with a husband. She is a loving, giving person who has found no other outlet for her need to be needed. And because of her poor self-image, Judy has sealed herself up in a little box and won't let anyone in.

Many single Christians have stepped forward recently to remind us that the single lifestyle can be as useful, happy, and dignified as married living. Some people are called to be single and are able to do more good in that state than if they were married. Their single lifestyle deserves respect.

But while we recognize the value of single living for some people, we should remember that married people do report greater happiness. Marriage is one of the few relationships where long-lasting intimacy with another person can be achieved, and where our deepest needs for affection and sexual enjoyment can be gratified. These benefits, rather than cultural conditioning, account for the greater happiness of many married people.

How can I make this statement when almost half of all first marriages in America end in divorce, and when so many young people are opting to live together without the benefit of that little piece of paper?

The high remarriage rate among the divorced (higher than the rate of first marriages) attests to the great benefits of marriage. Consider the experience of my friend Tess. Tess and Leon were married fifteen years and had one daughter, Laura. After the first few years, their interests changed until Laura was all they had in common. Leon was generally satisfied, but Tess became increasingly unhappy. It was nothing she could put her finger on . . . but Leon seemed so inconsiderate of her needs.

Tess found the men at work charming. Compared to her boss in his tailored suits, Leon seemed positively disgusting to Tess as he lounged before the TV with his pot belly stretching out his T-shirt.

Her divorced friends nurtured her discontent. "He takes you for granted. He doesn't appreciate you. You'll never reach your full potential saddled with him."

After sixteen years of marriage, Tess demanded a divorce. Leon was shocked; he had missed all the warning signs. "Why are you doing this? What do you want?"

"Freedom," Tess answered. "To be my own person. To develop my own potential. I can't live with you any more." She didn't want alimony, only child support for Laura, and mother and daughter moved into an apartment while Leon rattled around in the suddenly-too-big house.

A year later, Tess had second thoughts. "No, I don't want to go back with Leon . . . not after everything, but . . ." Her words came slowly, "I'm not as happy as I expected to be. I'm not even content."

"Why?" I prodded.

"I'm still lonely. My work, which I enjoy, isn't enough. And Laura . . . she resents me, and she has her own friends. We're not as close as we were before."

"Men in your life?"

She shrugged. "Don't they always say, 'the good ones are always married.' " Then she laughed. "I've had one close friendship, a divorced man at work, but it's ironic. He's unlike Leon in practically every way, but he has the same irritating habits." Silence again, then quietly, "Maybe I should have stayed married."

"Would you marry again?"

"Oh, sure, if I found the right man." Then she sobered instantly. "Maybe not, though. Maybe I'm the one who needs to change."

Sex Roles and Self-Esteem

I believe that marriage operates according to a set of laws given to us by God for our happiness and well-being. While reviewing research on marriage for my book *Sex Roles and the Christian Family*, I was struck by the fact that all studies pointed toward the biblical plan as the ideal blueprint for marriage.[3] Even slight departures from the biblical pattern have drastic and unpleasant effects both on society and on individual family members.

One of the most important laws upon which marriage operates is the law of complementarity—that two divergent natures must be blended into one. This law realizes that men and women have different roles to fill, different contributions to make.

At its most elementary level, complementarity between the sexes is illustrated in the "push-pull" principle. As elaborated by Dr. Charles Socarides, a New York State University psychiatrist, this principle unfolds in the act of intercourse. The sperm cells seek the egg, while at the same time the egg attracts the sperm. Thus male penetration acts as a pressure pump while the female response acts as a suction pump. "At the level of the total individual, the male seeks out, arouses, and penetrates the female. The female . . . attracts and embraces the male."[4]

This concept of push-pull complementarity effectively eliminates the old stereotype that men are "active" in sexual interchanges while women are "passive." Both sexes should be active, but in different ways. Women express their activity by drawing men to them—by creating the aura of love and support that pulls men in their direction. Men express their activity by seeking out and provoking this feminine activity.

The law of complementarity is an important source of

self-esteem in marriage, because it dictates that each partner make a unique contribution and fill a unique role. This doesn't mean that roles cannot or should not overlap. Rather, it affirms the dignity and importance of each partner's contribution.

I believe the husband-father has three primary roles.

1. *To provide for his family.*
2. *To stimulate his children's development.* Much has been learned about a father's contribution to his children's development. Children need their father's time and attention if they are to develop optimally.
3. *To use his leadership drive and aggressiveness to the benefit of his family.* We Christians would say that the father is to lead his family spiritually, to pray for them, and to be the priest of the family.

The wife-mother, on the other hand, has two primary roles.

1. *To give the home its warmth and attractiveness.* She does what the term "homemaker" implies: She turns a house into a home by associating herself with it. As I've stated elsewhere, her role is the pivotal point upon which the home revolves. Her nature and presence make it an attractive place for husband and children. Without her, the home becomes just a collection of sticks and bricks—a house.
2. *To train her children and to provide an atmosphere of love* and nurture in which they can grow up with a sense of security, a feeling of belonging, and an affection for home and family.

Complementary Sex Roles

The fact that husbands and wives have a different set of *primary* roles affirms the unique contribution that each makes. Cultures that follow a pattern of complementary roles are generally much stronger than those that depart from it. As a matter of fact, the further a society departs from complementary sex roles, the less chance it has of surviving.

Anthropologist Margaret Mead was one of the first social

scientists to observe clearly the importance of complementary sex roles to a society's strength and effectiveness. Based upon her extensive work among many different cultures, both primitive and advanced, she concluded that "if any human society . . . is to survive, it must have a pattern of social life that comes to terms with the differences between the sexes."[5]

In other words, all societies must set up appropriate sex roles and agree on what is expected of men and women. Those roles must allow for the differences between the sexes by recognizing the different contributions men and women make. Societies that don't properly deal with those differences, Mead observed, wouldn't likely last for very long.

Throughout history, women generally have done a much better job of filling their sex roles than men have done in meeting their own. It's a sad observation, but still true, that men are quicker to desert their roles than women.

I recall a disheartening telephone conversation with a young Christian mother. She worked for a company I was doing business with. She called me to discuss a technical matter, and during our conversation she suddenly said: "Dr. Blitchington, I wanted to tell you that I read your book, and I agree one hundred percent with what you said about the importance of the father's contribution to his children's development."

Beaming, I started to thank her. But what I heard next made me gulp instead.

"My husband left me for another woman about three years ago," she continued, "and I've had to raise our three children by myself. They really miss their father. I can tell that it's hurt their development."

This is not the sort of conversation that makes a pro-family writer feel very good. I can hold up the ideal, the high standards for Christian families to live by, but all too often I see the practical realities created by frail human nature.

Fortunately, this young woman was able to keep a sense of perspective and a positive attitude despite her less-than-ideal situation. She didn't wallow in guilt, heaping all the blame for her misfortune on herself, as many women in the same situation are tempted to do. Neither did she over-emphasize her husband's sin, as bad as it was. Rather, she owned up to her failings as a wife, received forgiveness, and attempted to make a bad situation as positive as possible. She didn't let it gnaw on her self-esteem.

The law of complementarity is a powerful force, affirming as it does the unique contribution each partner makes to the family. In one sense, it enhances each partner's self-esteem by spelling out that unique contribution. "I am not complete without you," it leads each partner to say. "I need you to round me out, to make up for that which I lack."

This is in line with God's plan. Everything in creation is designed to avoid self-sufficiency. The earth needs the seed, the seed needs the earth. Human beings need each other. God never intended for them to stand alone.

This mutual dependency draws us together and, at the same time, makes us very vulnerable. Our need for the other gives the other power to hurt us. It's reassuring to know that each of us has a unique role in the home, yet it's frightening to realize that our unique contribution can be trampled upon or our partner's unique contribution taken from us.

Men suffer from this feeling of vulnerability no less than women. In fact, men are probably more insecure about their roles than women are. Husbands typically need a period in which they first establish themselves in their role as provider. Then they are better able to encourage their wives to develop their own talents. This is especially true when children come, for the children almost always attach themselves to the mother more than to the father. This affirms her importance, but at the same time it calls his into question. He is able to reaffirm his contribution to the family through his role as provider.

These insecurities over sex role compatibility seem to manifest themselves daily. Sometimes they are precipitated by rapid social changes. Sometimes they result from new ideologies. Sometimes they simply evolve naturally as a couple's family situation changes.

That's what happened to Tom and Lorna. Their twenty-year marriage had produced two healthy children and a fairly comfortable financial lifestyle from Tom's job as a truck driver. Lorna had stayed home until the last child left the nest, faithfully fulfilling her homemaking and maternal roles. Now that her children were gone and the home was empty most of the day, she was ready to extend her energies into the world of work. She wanted to attend college, work on a degree in elementary education, and eventually teach school—an ambition she had had since adolescence.

Tom was crushed when she announced her new goals. He had become accustomed to her presence in the home and, although he knew his reactions were unreasonable, he couldn't help but interpret her new desire as a lack of appreciation for all those years he had supported the family. He felt like his contribution was being threatened. Consequently, a marriage once blessed by contentment was filled now with tension.

What would you say to this couple if you were their marriage counselor? Was Tom being unreasonable in allowing his self-esteem to be so affected by his wife's desire to develop her talents? I've found that men in this situation are afraid that their wives are going to grow away from them. The couple has worked together for years in a pattern of sex-role complementarity, and now he fears she is going to disturb that pattern. She now has the resources and time to move in a new direction, while he is still bound by his job and his role as provider. He fears they will be pulled apart and that the life they had will be lost.

The problem of uncomplementary sex roles is occurring with increasing frequency in America; even those who once advocated sexual equality are having second thoughts about the trend. Sociologist Jesse Bernard recently observed that men are deserting the "good provider" role. "Some feel their efforts have not been appreciated by their families," she laments.

The law of complementarity is crucial to the interests of

any society, but it can't insure the happiness and satisfaction of individual men and women *unless the complementary roles are given equal respect and dignity*. If both sexes are to gain self-esteem and genuine satisfaction from their respective roles, then those roles must be seen as equally important and valuable. But, as pointed out earlier, the male role has been given the greater amount of importance. This is one reason more and more women are choosing it.

When separate sex roles are given equal respect and dignity, the law of complementarity makes unity between husband and wife possible. From a theoretical standpoint this seems simple and straightforward. All we have to do is train men to assume the provider role aggressively, and women to care for the home and children. But in practice, this issue of complementary sex roles is much more complicated than that.

Feminists such as Betty Friedan have observed that modern labor-saving devices enable women to devote a much smaller portion of their time to household activities than they used to. Further, the new technology has transferred many jobs—the manufacture of clothing, for example—from the home to the factory. These changes have taken away from many women a source of domestic activity and productivity.

Jobs have become more than just a way of earning money; today they are looked upon as providing a source of contact with the outside world, a channel through which individual talents can be identified and developed, and a way of adding structure to one's existence in an oftentimes unstructured and confusing world.

Finally, many women simply *have* to work; they have no choice in the matter. Some are deserted by irresponsible husbands; others have to bring home a second paycheck to keep the family financially secure. Many women work before children are born and after the last child leaves home (or enters school).

All these factors must be taken into consideration before we harden the law of complementarity into a rigid mold, for modern society requires flexibility amid changing circumstances. What may be ideal in one culture or at one point in time may become less desirable in another culture or era. The Bible contains a framework for family living, but there is room for some change within that framework. At the same time, we should never conclude that the biblical laws of family living are outmoded or culture-specific.

So, although we call for flexible sex roles, we should avoid going beyond the limits of the laws that determine optimum sex-role adjustments. The strength and stability of family and society are at stake, as is the happiness of both women and men.

There is evidence that America has already deviated beyond the realm of healthy, complementary sex roles. There is further evidence that we are beginning to reap the fruits of this deviation.

One of the first persons to observe the new trend toward non-complementary (or egalitarian) sex roles was George Gilder. In his best-selling book, *Sexual Suicide,* Gilder observed "a growing and influential trend toward a masculinized female" and a "feminized male." The final result of this loss of distinctive roles and personalities, he predicted, would be a generation of men and women whose personalities would no longer be compatible.

> Because sexuality is normally fulfilled in complementary relationship to the opposite sex, this generation of "human beings" has deep trouble achieving the deep sexual connections on which human identity and male socialization depend. Partly because of economic trends, the male, once an obsessive provider who gave everything but himself, is losing his career orientation. Partly because of the change in the male, the obsessive mother is giving way to the obsolescent mother. The future of love and family is in the balance.[6]

The future of love and marriage has already been called into question in Sweden. That country has carried the cause of sexual equality further than any other nation. Let's look a bit closer at the Swedish experiment with traditional, complementary sex roles.

Swedish authorities recognized that if women were to be given true equality, the government would have to force men legally to treat women as they would treat men. Men would have to be compelled to undertake traditional female domestic tasks and women would have to be forced to undertake the traditional male provider role. In a 1968 "Report to the United Nations," Swedish authorities formally stated that "the aim of reform . . . must be to change the traditional division of labor which tends to deprive women of the possibility of exercising their legal rights on equal terms."[7]

So laws were passed to ensure that "Swedish men would be *required* to assume a greater share of responsibility for the upbringing of children and household chores." Women were no longer to be supported economically in marriage, and "the husband's traditional obligation to support his wife was modified to constitute a shared responsibility with her for the support of the children." This new change was made possible by the creation of government-subsidized day-care centers to look after the young children involved.

The results of this experiment with egalitarianism have been devastating to the Swedish family. It would be hard to say who has been damaged the most—the women or the children. Swedish children, raised in day-care centers without stable contact with their mothers, grow up lacking self-esteem.

This is consistent with the findings of such day-care observers as psychiatrist Marie Meierhofer, who studied the effects of government-sponsored day-care in such socialist countries as Switzerland. She concluded that "socialist countries, and some western ones, in which children have been herded in nurseries at an early age while their mothers work, are beginning to see the fundamental error in their system of child care."[8] The five hundred day-care children she filmed in Zurich nurseries showed frequent depressions, low activity level, apathy, and fear.

There is some indication that girls are hurt more by this arrangement than boys. Psychiatrist Herbert Hendin studied the results of the new Swedish practices and reported those results in his book *Suicide and Scandinavia*. He found that separating children from their mothers creates anger and deflates self-esteem.[9] Swedish men and women who grew up in day-care centers suffer a deficit in self-esteem that could possibly be softened by clinging to one another for support in marriage. But the new Swedish sex-role laws make it so hard for men and women to genuinely love and need one another that most of the benefits of traditional, complementary marriage are denied them. In fact, marriage has lost so much of its attraction that Swedish men avoid it like the plague. Illegitimacy and cohabitation are rampant in Sweden.

But the problems don't stop there. Swedish women are not happy with their new independence. One of the best indicators of personal happiness and self-esteem is the suicide rate. Dr. Hendin found that during this time of sex-role changes, the suicide rate among Swedish women increased more than any other nation's. It is more than one and a half times that of United States women. The failure of marriage and the disruption of complementary sex roles— upon which the family is built—prevent women from developing healthy self-esteem and a feeling of security and personal identity.

The Ideal Versus Practical Reality

It's always easier to lift up a high ideal than it is to live it. I've described what I see as the ideal for marriage and family living, but every day I see women (and men) who are unable to meet these standards through no fault of their own. Economic conditions make it difficult for some couples to achieve these ideals. Inflation eats away at their savings. The husband is unable to support the family with his income alone. He could take a part-time job in the evenings, but that might be more harmful to the family than if his wife went to work, since children need contact with their fathers, too.

Families caught in this dilemma can't afford to let guilt and anxiety spoil the time they do have with their children. It could be, as some people suggest, that social and economic conditions will enforce a new pattern of marital roles upon us, no matter what we do. But I believe that Christians have a duty to continue to uphold the ideal, even when it becomes impossible to achieve in all its particulars. The danger is that we might lose sight of the ideal altogether.

I believe God created men and women differently for a purpose. If, as I suggest, our happiness and self-esteem are promoted by these complementary roles and interchanges, then we would be well advised not to turn our backs upon these ideals. The danger is that changing social conditions and new ideologies will cause us to lose sight of those deeper drives, feelings, and experiences that make us feel good about ourselves as men and women.

Indications are that the movement away from complementary sex-role relationships is not as fulfilling as once thought. Betty Friedan—the main impetus behind the current feminist movement—recently documented this change in the modern woman's orientation.

In 1963, Friedan described in *The Feminine Mystique* how some modern women were questioning the traditional roles of wife and mother, which they had been trained to devote themselves to. She wrote that the main question women in traditional roles asked themselves was, "Is this all?"

"That's how the modern Women's Movement began," Friedan asserts, "with new questions." Those questions (and Friedan's book) inspired a spate of books and articles devoted to the idea that women should find their happiness and self-esteem apart from men, children, and the family.

But in a recent *Redbook* magazine article, Betty Friedan describes a new set of questions that modern women are asking. "Talking to young women all over the country this past year, I realized that the new opportunities, the new options and choices, have created a new set of problems."[10]

Increasing numbers of anxious, harassed women are asking Friedan questions like, "Is it really true, that business of 'it's the quality, not the quantity, of time you spend with your children'?" "How can I have the kind of marriage I want and the kind of career I want, and be a good mother?'' ''Why can't I just stay home, be a mother, and enjoy it?''

Another young woman—a medical doctor—told Friedan that she thought she could have a medical career, a marriage, and children. But ''now that I'm in this very demanding profession, which I love, I wonder. Maybe I can't have it all.''

One young homemaker felt pressured to go back to business school. She has no interest in finance, but she dreads being asked ''What do you do?'' at parties. ''Even if you're doing what you want to do, mainly taking care of your own kids, more and more you're the odd woman out.''

A woman who works in a bank told Friedan her husband had assumed more responsibility in the home and with the children since she had gone back to work. But despite this supposedly ideal setup, she felt dissatisfied with her life. ''You have to make it in a man's world, doing it their way. I don't like what it's doing to me.''

''What it's doing to me. What it's doing to my family. What it's doing to my children.'' These are the complaints one hears more and more frequently among today's women. To be sure, some women like the new sex-role arrangements. But many others feel those non-complementary relationships are hostile to the family, to children, and to the happiness and self-esteem of the women caught up in them.

Women and Work: Some Suggestions

The question of when, and to what extent, a wife should work outside the home is complex and sensitive. The welfare of children must be taken into consideration. They may not acquire the character, self-esteem, and love of home and family living they need if they are whisked off to a nursery or day-care center for eight to ten hours a day during their formative years. It is the fortunate working mother who can find a loving, homelike atmosphere for her preschoolers and a sitter who supports her discipline.

The warmth and attractiveness of the home is another issue. The home revolves around the woman; she gives it its heart. Without the presence of a loving mother to comfort and prod, the home usually becomes less attractive. Husband and children are likely to seek gratification outside the family.

Finally, the wife must support her husband's role as leader of the family. In the past, the husband's role as provider reinforced his role as leader. However, with increasing numbers of working wives, there is a great ambivalence over just who is in charge of the family. Children can feel adrift without their mother at home to give their lives stability and without their father as the clearcut head of the home.

On the other side of the ledger, there are the needs mentioned earlier: the need of women to participate in the world of work, the need to develop other sides of the personality, the need to structure time, to feel competent, and often to supplement a husband's income. In view of these sometimes conflicting needs, I would like to offer the following suggestions for those who wish to find the best answer to this question of sexual roles and work.

1. It is very important for a mother to be home with her children during the preschool years if at all possible. A day-care center is not usually an ideal place for children to spend more than half of their waking hours. Also, we Christians must seize every opportunity to train our children for Christ. That takes time.

2. Part-time jobs are the best compromise for the woman who either wants to work or has to work but who still has small children in the home. One study found that wives with part-time jobs were more satisfied than wives who had full-time jobs. This is the type of arrangement Solomon recommends in Proverbs 31—the famous "virtuous woman" chapter. This woman weaves wool and flax and sells it in the market. This part-time job, apparently conducted in the home, is a secondary aspect of her role, not the primary aspect. The fact that part-time jobs are not

available to many women is evidence that industry must adapt to the needs of women who don't want outside work to dominate their time.

3. The most destructive working arrangement to the family is a careerist orientation among wives. Studies have shown that highly committed career women have the second highest divorce rate of all groups investigated.[11] The only group with a higher divorce rate are those on welfare— the poverty-stricken. A careerist orientation among wives affects every part of the marital relationship. For example, *McCall's* magazine recently reported the results of a questionnaire on marriage that some twenty thousand women responded to.[12] Of all the women who responded, those with the greatest amount of career involvement also had the most complaints about their marital relationships. They even seemed less happy with their own lives at work, listing "job stress" as one of their most gnawing problems.

4. Don't blame yourself if you simply cannot reach the ideal in all its particulars. If you have small children but are forced to work because of financial conditions, the worst thing you could do is feel guilty and allow your self-esteem to suffer because of it. I believe God will grant us His help when we find ourselves in these circumstances. Often, with His strength added to our efforts, we can bring forth optimal results from less-than-ideal situations. God loves you and stands ready to help you when you ask. You can count on that.

Six

Six Types of
Marital Relationships

In the last chapter we looked at evidence demonstrating the myth of the egalitarian marriage. Stable families are built upon complementary, divergent husband-wife roles, not upon equality or sameness. Complementarity, one of the most basic family laws, states that both partners bring something unique to the marriage.

But the law of complementarity goes beyond sex roles. Masculinity complements femininity; the male brain complements the female brain; male aggressiveness and leadership complement female empathy and nurture.

These are very general and fundamental laws of marriage. On a more specific level, even personalities are attuned to the law of complementarity, at least in successful marriages. Ever since the publication of Robert Winch's classic book, *Mate Selection,* psychologists have recognized the truth behind the aphorism "opposites attract."[1] Winch found that for every important need of one spouse in a successful marriage, the other spouse had the opposite need. Persons with a high need for dominance marry mates with a high need for submissiveness, for example. This provides a balance in the marriage; each spouse is able to draw upon the other's strength.

This complementary balance exists in most strong marriages. Our constant exposure to the myth of rugged individualism in this country prevents us from realizing how much we need one another, especially in marriage. To have a successful marriage, each mate must find in the other what he lacks in himself. Ecclesiastes 4:9 clearly describes the importance of this principle of marriage: "Two can accomplish more than twice as much as one, for the results can be much better. If one falls, the other pulls him up; but if a man falls when he is alone, he's in trouble" (TLB). No doubt this was why Christ sent His disciples out in pairs.

Every personality has both strengths and weaknesses. But for almost every one of our personality weaknesses, some member of the opposite sex has a corresponding set of strengths. Somehow we recognize that that person has what we lack, and we are drawn to him or her. The larger unit that we form with our mates is stronger, healthier, more resourceful, and happier than anything we could have achieved alone.

One great danger is that you might fail to realize the important contribution you make to your spouse and fall into self-depreciation. Or you might fail to appreciate the important influence your spouse has on you, thus leading to dissatisfaction with the marriage. Another danger is that the weaknesses of one partner will become so overwhelming that the other will be unable or unwilling to provide compensatory strengths.

In order to promote better understanding and appreciation of the important role this principle plays, I'd like to describe six types of complementary marital arrangements. These six types are not meant to exhaust all possible combinations of personality styles among married couples, but they do seem to be the main ones.

As you read about these complementary marital patterns, think about the kind of people you typically form relationships with. I believe that friendships, as well as marriages, follow this pattern of complementarity. Think about how the self-esteem of each partner is affected by the personality, needs, and behaviors of the other, as each partner tries to define himself or herself through the eyes of the spouse.

The Hypomanic—Depressive Marriage

According to psychotherapist and marriage counselor Dr. David Klimek, this is the most general and pervasive complementary marriage.[2] All the others, he says, contain elements of this pattern.

"Hypomanic" means "less than manic." A person with a hypomanic personality is energetic, confident, optimistic, and bold. His liveliness, talkativeness, and sociable nature make him enjoyable to be with. His enthusiasm and zest for living make it easy for him to tackle difficult tasks. In general, hypomanic persons do not seem anxious or insecure on the surface. But if you look closer, you'll find that they simply handle their anxieties through activity.

Theodore Roosevelt was a prime example of the hypomanic personality. He was always active, energetic, ebullient, and optimistic. Henry Cabot Lodge wrote that "his mere presence was so full of vitality, so charged with energy, that it was contagious, and seemed to bring all the possible joy of living as a gift or rather as an atmosphere to those who rode or walked beside him."

Roosevelt's energy was amazing. He often worked until late in the night, writing letters, books, and memoirs, and studying up on the special interests of his guests so he would be able to talk about subjects they liked. His ability to lead and inspire is famous. He could persuade people to take any kind of risk with his infectious energy and enthusiasm. Many historians believe he was the greatest politician and hardest worker of his time.

You can easily get the impression that people with a hypomanic personality are so competent and energetic that they have few faults. Such is not the case. These people have glaring weaknesses that only a spouse of the opposite temperament can compensate for. Roosevelt had all the strengths *and* weaknesses of the hypomanic, and he married a woman who could bring a balance to his personality.

In the first place, Roosevelt was so excitable and impatient that his early political career was almost a failure. He was very inconsiderate of the feelings of subordinates, and he made several enemies because of his cruelty and arrogance. One British visitor described Roosevelt as "an interesting combination of St. Vitus and St. Paul."

One of Roosevelt's most serious weaknesses, and the one that afflicts almost all hypomanics, was a lack of judgment. His impulsiveness, excitability, and arrogance sometimes prompted him to make poor judgments. When Roosevelt retired from the presidency, he became a candidate for the presidency of Harvard University. But he was turned down because, in the words of one of the trustees, "We need a man of judgment, and is judgment to be found coupled with such enormous energy?"

To a large extent, this man's observation was accurate. Hypomanic personalities have tremendous energy and drive, but sometimes at the expense of good judgment. That's why they are attracted to calm, placid mates who are much less energetic and much less impulsive.

Roosevelt was no exception. His attraction to mild-mannered Alice Lee is significant. This very stable woman often discouraged Roosevelt's impetuous drive, which probably saved him much embarrassment. Psychiatrist Ronald Fieve, in his excellent book entitled *Moodswing,* described the impact Alice Lee had upon Roosevelt.

> Roosevelt's attraction to this calm girl illustrates once again the tendency of hypomanics to be attracted to and to marry people whom they can control . . . but who often turn out to be their salvation, because of their slower, steadier pace and their more realistic judgment.[3]

This quote confirms the important role the hypomanic's spouse—the "depressive partner"—plays in the relationship. Hypomanics are prone to doing things without thinking them through. They buy things they don't need, take too many risks, or make impulsive decisions. The depressive mate adds a balancing factor. His (or her) more cautious, calm, reasonable nature helps shield the hypomanic from his own impulsivity by emphasizing rational, rather than emotional, decision-making.

I once counseled a young "hypomanic" graduate student and his "depressive" wife. When he was two thirds of the way through his doctoral program, he had an impulse to add another year's worth of courses onto his program. When he tried to discuss it with his wife, she quickly threw cold water onto his plans. She had already been waiting several years for him to complete his work and get his Ph.D., and she didn't want to wait another year. It was a case of his energy and enthusiasm against her calm rationality. That's when they came to me. My job was to help him see the logic behind his wife's resistance. Together, we all decided that the best approach was for him to go ahead and get his degree. Then, after he had a job, he could take any extra courses he wanted.

While the depressive partner has a calming effect on his or her spouse, the hypomanic's energy and enthusiasm add life and joy to the depressive's existence. Without an outgoing hypomanic partner, the depressive person's life would be dull and sad. By respecting one another's gifts and contributions, the two spouses insure each other's self-esteem. By pooling their resources, the two make a stronger, more effective unit.

"Just what does she see in him?" everyone asked when outgoing, vivacious Nikkie married low-key, unexcitable Matt. But when the honeymoon lengthened into months and then the first anniversary came, we realized they were happy. Nikkie needed to achieve and be admired, and Matt gave her what she needed. He encouraged her in her diverse volunteer work, and obviously found a quiet joy when she landed a part in a local theatre production. We also observed that she drew him out in conversations, and he wasn't the dull fellow we'd thought him to be. Matt and Nikkie have grown together, and both lives have been enriched.

Many amateur psychologists make the mistake of assuming that the hypomanic partner, because of his friendly nature, is healtheir than the depressive mate. This is untrue. Each is "healthy" in some ways and "unhealthy" in other ways.

Another common mistake is to assume that the depressive partner needs the hypomanic spouse more than he or she is needed. Depressive people *do* seem to need an intimate one-to-one relationship, while hypomanics can get by with several superficial or casual relationships. But the hypomanic actually craves recognition and attention more than the depressive. In a well-functioning marriage, the hypomanic thrives under his depressive spouse's admiration.

The two need one another. If two hypomanics marry, too much competition for the spotlight impairs the relationship. If two depressives wed, the relationship is listless and dull.

Of course, the hypomanic-depressive marriage, like the other complementary relationships, can go sour. The partners can fail to understand or appreciate the special gifts the other spouse brings to the relationship. The hypomanic husband's energy can be turned against his wife in the form of bullying if he becomes overly frustrated. Sometimes the depressive spouse withholds the approval and appreciation the hypomanic partner craves, and the hypomanic partner retaliates by turning to extramarital affairs. The depressive partner can become overly cautious and critical, or the hypomanic spouse can ignore his mate's contribution, preferring to make all the decisions himself. The marriage can lose its balance if either partner's negative traits become too strong, or if the positive traits become too weak to balance out the other's negative traits.

Because communication is so important to a marriage, novice marriage counselors sometimes make the mistake of assuming that if they just teach a couple the art of communication, everything else will take care of itself. This is not necessarily true. Unless the two partners really appreciate their collective gifts, communication may cause a stalemate in the marriage. And unless each partner makes an effort to grow—to control the weaknesses and develop the strengths of his own personality style—communication may be an exercise in futility.

Creative Obsessive—Administrative Optimist

This complementary marriage is a variation of the hypomanic-depressive relationship. Here the husband is somewhat shy, introverted, and detached while his wife is outgoing, warm, optimistic, and enthusiastic.

Several years ago my wife and I became acquainted with a couple who closely fit this pattern. Alice and Wyatt were an attractive couple in their early thirties, with two children. The outstanding factor in their relationship was Alice's energy and joy of living. She enthusiastically jumped into any new activity and agreeably undertook any task, from teaching a church class to keeping children for sick mothers. Her husband was opposite in temperament. He was very hard to get to know and was anything but eager to tackle new tasks or make new friends. In fact, sometimes he seemed irritable and grouchy, ridiculing his wife or snapping at her for not attending to some detail of importance to him.

Gail and Joey are another couple who make one wonder how they got together. They were from a small town, and neither of them dated much. Gail says that when she saw Joey, she said, "I want to go with that guy." She is tall and dark, with a quick mind and a snappy temper, while Joey is tall, fair, and completely unflappable.

Joey works in a factory and operates a good-sized farm on the side. Gail feeds the calves and picks the corn and sells it on the market. Both are intelligent. But perhaps because of his reticent manner, Joey seems duller than vivacious Gail.

"I was terribly lonely the first years," Gail confides. "Joey would come home, and I'd yell and shout up one wall and down the other. You know Joey . . . he never gets mad." She laughs. "That just takes the steam out of my anger."

They've been married thirteen years. Now that their youngest is in school, Gail is going to college. She's always wanted to be a children's counselor.

What does Joey say? "Oh, he doesn't care. He's happy for me to have a chance to find out if this is what I really want." She smiles and her whole face lights up. "I'm really very lucky to have him."

In this type of marriage, however, the men run a danger of becoming cynical. A thread of pessimism and despair runs through their very appearance. Often they turn their negative attitude onto their wives, deriding the women for their enthusiasm and joy. The interaction between Archie and Edith Bunker of *All in the Family* fame illustrates this tendency. Archie was forever turning his sharp wit against Edith's enthusiasm and good will, calling her a "dingbat" and sneering at her joy of living.

These men often appear ungrateful and churlish. But what's usually hidden from view is their desperate need for their wives' optimism and good spirits to counteract their own pessimism and despair. The men in this type of relationship have an almost unbearable need to experience happiness, spontaneity, and a childlike joy of living, but they are unable to do so because of their naturally pessimistic dispositions. *So they experience their joy and happiness through their wives.* Even as he cynically ridicules his wife for her "unwillingness to see reality," the pessimistic husband desperately needs to believe there really is something enjoyable in life. In a sense, he lives through her.

There's a tendency to view the woman in this type of marriage as healthy and the men as sick. In fact, some marriage counselors actually believe the wives would do much better if they could just get rid of their husbands. This is untrue. The husbands in this type of marriage have gifts to contribute, also.

In the first place, these men usually have creative, original minds. Their sensitivity makes them alert and receptive to new ideas and impressions—one of the most important factors behind artistic creativity and originality. But that same sensitivity makes them susceptible to pain, rudeness, and mistreatment from others. In a sense, they need to be shielded from intrusions from the outside world. And their wives usually perform this task—monitoring calls, dealing with repairmen and visitors, and such.

I've called these men "creative obsessives" because of their tendency to become wrapped up in ideas and intellectual pursuits, if they have considerably more education than Archie Bunker. The stereotype of this kind of marriage is the obsessional scientist who is absorbed in some creative project while his wife takes care of all the practical areas. In fact, it's amazing to see how many scientists have had this type of marriage. Henry Ford, Thomas Edison, Charles H. Cooley, and E. E. Thorndike were all "creative obsessives" married to energetic, optimistic women who took care of the administrative aspects of their lives.

A second gift this type of man possesses is an ability to perceive details and to view things objectively without interference from emotion. This objectivity makes them good scientists, and their alertness to detail enables them to be accountants or mathematicians. But these same gifts can turn into liabilities as well (as can most gifts). Their objectivity can make them detached and aloof. Their lack of emotion can deprive them of experiences such as joy and happiness. And their ability to perceive details can make them overly critical. They need their optimistic wives to balance out these negative traits.

But what many people fail to see is that these wives also need their husband's assets. These optimistic women eagerly plunge into any new activity that comes their way, often leaving behind a string of unfinished tasks.

Margie was always excited about something. Whether starting a nursery school, painting the kitchen, or planning a trip, her enthusiasm knew no bounds. But once the project was underway, she lost interest. Her friends knew it was useless to count on her to follow through.

Their husbands go to the other extreme. They stick with one pursuit, often ignoring the odds-and-ends of everyday practical living. The obsessive husband's one-track mind complements his wife's "shotgun" approach.

The optimism and enthusiasm of this type of wife can be carried to an extreme. She can become overly idealistic, making decisions on the basis of emotion rather than reason. She often develops the Scarlett O'Hara attitude that things will always work out tomorrow. She gets by on blind optimism. Her husband's approach is much more realistic. He sees the problems and conflicts of life and tries to prepare for them. Together, they are able to grapple with all problems. Her idealism is complemented by his realism.

This type of marriage can be impaired when the husband becomes so overburdened by his pessimism and cynicism that he tries to avoid reality altogether. One husband turns to alcohol; another spends all his spare time in front of a TV set. In this case, both partners fail to develop their intellectual gifts.

In a well-functioning complementary marriage involving these personality types, the negative traits are not allowed to dominate the relationship. In a mature marriage, husbands and wives recognize their own strengths and weaknesses, along with those of their mates. Their self-esteem is promoted, rather than impaired, when each recognizes and appreciates the unique contribution the other makes.

The Moody—Stable Marriage

When you find a marriage in which one partner is moody, the other partner is almost always emotionally stable. Marriages between two moody persons usually don't last long. (Marriages between two emotionally even-tempered people may last a long time, but are often dull.)

Whenever one mate is subject to swings and shifts in mood, in order for complementarity to exist the other mate should be even-tempered and stable. Marriages between persons who differ in emotional stability can take place on several levels.

At one level, the emotionally unstable person may actually be manic-depressive. This term refers to a person who has extreme emotional highs and lows. When he's high, he resembles the hypomanic. He's charming, outgoing, talkative, energetic, and confident. But then he comes crashing down into a depressed state. His emotions change completely, and he experiences despair, listlessness, and sadness. Then all of a sudden his mood rises, and he returns to a state of mania. Thus the cycle continues.

Psychiatrist Ronald Fieve reports the case of an executive who underwent predictable forty-eight hour cycles. For two days he would work very hard, confidently laying plans and making decisions.Then, for the next two days, he would be in a state of extreme depression. His secretary would often have to cancel all his appointments, as he was too dispirited to work.[4]

According to Dr. Fieve, Winston Churchill had a manic-depressive personality. During his highs, he closely resembled Theodore Roosevelt, with his energy, drive, and confidence. But unlike Roosevelt, who was almost always buoyant in mood, Churchill experienced periodic deep depressions. Early in his life, Churchill had been predominantly manic in mood, but during the 1930s he became depressed, cautious, and uncertain. His mood elevated during the war years, though, and he was able to use his energy to inspire the British people with courage. Not surprisingly, Churchill married a very stable woman, whose easygoing emotional nature compensated for his inconsistent emotional pattern.

In a sense, the spouse of a manic-depressive person has to have two qualities: emotional stability *and* supportiveness. The supportiveness is necessary when confronting a person who at times is energetic and confident, but who now is depressed and uncertain. To a manic-depressive, an easygoing spouse is an island of stability and predictability in an unstable emotional world.

On a second level, the moody spouse may not be as extreme as a manic-depressive. He or she may be subject to mood swings in the normal, rather than severe, range.

Abraham Lincoln is a good example of the mildly moody person. In fact, his life history provides a good illustration of the need for complementarity in the marital relationship and what happens when that complementarity is not present.

Lincoln's mood swings are common knowledge. He would go through periods when he was very optimistic and outgoing, often spending hours telling jokes and stories. Then he would withdraw into despair. His first fiancée, Ann Rutledge, was apparently a very easygoing, stable woman—the sort of person a moody individual needs. But after her death, he married Mary Todd—an ambitious, energetic woman who was herself fairly unstable emotionally. As a result of this mismatch, the Lincolns had a very unhappy married life.

On a third level, the moody spouse may actually be more positive and upbeat than the stable partner, who is calm but self-effacing. Usually the unstable partner in this type of marriage is characterized by hostile silences and resentments, rather than depressions. One couple I know consists of a somewhat arrogant wife who takes her frustrations and resentments out on family members, and her easygoing husband, who provides the family with stability. The wife's constant dissatisfaction is countered by the husband's contentment and calmness.

These marriages between emotional opposites can work well if the moody spouse doesn't let his emotions get completely out of control, and if the stable spouse doesn't tire of his partner's emotional swings. The important thing is that both partners recognize what each brings to the marriage and how one partner's personality is rounded out by the other.

Happy-Go-Lucky Man—Compulsive Woman

When I first began my college teaching career, I developed a friendship with Joe and Jennie, an interesting couple who typify this type of marriage. Both were very attractive. Joe was tall, blond, and bearded. Jennie was a short, slender brunette.

Joe's sociable, entertaining personality dominated the marriage. If ever anyone deserved the title "life-of-the-party," it was Joe. He was so much fun to be with that a salesman I knew took Joe with him on many of his business trips. He just naturally put the salesman's clients in a positive frame of mind.

Jennie was opposite in temperament. Quiet, shy, and reserved, she was a good complement to Joe. Almost every other girl Joe dated had fallen easily for his charm and good looks. Jennie was the first to keep control of herself. Perhaps that's one reason Joe was attracted to her—she wasn't a pushover.

At first, their marriage was strengthened by their complementary balance of traits. Joe ran his own business, doing woodwork in homes. Jennie managed both Joe and the books. Her compulsive nature and desire to keep things under control kept Joe from giving in to his more irresponsible impulses.

After about two years, though, the marriage started to weaken. Joe had trouble settling down and assuming responsibility. His spiritual life was a series of deep backslides followed by enthusiastic repentances, followed by even deeper backslides. Jennie was self-righteous and even somewhat contemptuous, rather than forgiving and loving. Soon they broke up for good.

A marriage between a "life-of-the-party" man and a quiet, compulsive woman can work well if the weaknesses don't get out of hand. The man will usually be somewhat distractible and impulsive. He will tend to be carried along by whatever the group is doing (one reason why these men need to watch their associations). He will also tend to forget appointments and overlook some responsibilities. That's okay, as long as he doesn't go too far. His more compulsive wife can compensate for these weaknesses by reminding, prodding, and alerting her more forgetful mate.

Sometimes problems arise because of the wife's weaknesses. One of the more frequent trouble areas is emotional coldness. Compulsive women can draw away from their husbands, failing to give them the love and recognition they crave. Or they can become so concerned with managerial activities that they forget about the relationship. Finally, they can become self-righteous and contemptuous, as Jennie did.

I watched the results of this type of marriage in a neighbor's family. The husband was a very easygoing man who never met a stranger. His wife was compulsive and controlling. His affable nature led to a very good public-relations job in a large corporation. As his wife became more domineering at home, he turned more and more toward work. As he became wrapped up in his job, she turned her attention to their slightly retarded son. She began babying him. She shaved him, pampered him, fed him, and directed his life, even when he was well into his thirties. When she and her husband died, the son was so spoiled and difficult to deal with that several institutions expelled him, and no relatives wanted any part of him.

A marriage of this nature doesn't have to end sadly, although it often does. If the husband is willing to assume leadership and responsibility in his home, and if his wife is willing to encourage his leadership attempts, both can grow and profit from the relationship. She can take care of the details, and he can give her the spontaneity and fun her temperament lacks.

That's the type of relationship Ed Simpson and his wife Peggy have. He is a policeman; she runs a day-care center in their home and cares for their two children. At first glance, you'd think Ed and Peggy have a marriage of similar personalities. Both are lively, outgoing, and cheerful. You have to invite them over at least three weeks in advance, for they're booked solid that far ahead of time.

Ed is the entertainer. He keeps everyone in stitches with his police stories and lively wit. Peggy is quieter, but she still laughs, jokes, and holds her own.

Their different temperaments and complementary relationship show up when you get to know them well. Ed brings joy and sociability into Peggy's life (and to everyone around him). Peggy takes care of details. She prompts Ed, reminding him of what needs to be done, warning him when his behavior gets out of hand. Ed takes it good-naturedly. He allows himself to be made more conscientious. And he takes responsibility for family leadership.

Neither Ed nor Peggy is thin-skinned. Each appreciates, rather than resents, the other's contribution. As a result, their self-esteem is promoted through their interactions with one another. Their marriage is strong and fulfilling.

The Economic Man—Supportive Woman

In a sense, this type of marriage is the opposite of the one above. The husband is aggressive, controlling, and compulsive. His wife is easygoing and relaxed. He manipulates her, which is easy because she likes to be led.

Nate and Minnie are a good example of the negatives of this type of marriage. Nate is a hard-working career man who quickly rose to the top in a difficult field. His wife was supportive all the way, often taking some of Nate's home responsibilities upon herself so he would be free to advance his career.

Like many of these men, Nate had a very economic view of human relationships. He believed in such aphorisms as "tit-for-tat" and "It's a dog-eat-dog world." This made him appear very hard-boiled. As a boss, he drove his employees and himself relentlessly. He seemed to evaluate everyone, including his wife and children, according to what kind of services they could provide. This cold emphasis upon work, and his lack of warmth, cast much tension and gloom over the household. As a result, both his children had academic troubles in school. They seemed to lack motivation and desire. And they also liked to get out of the house, away from their father.

This kind of marriage often suffers because the father only interacts with his family in a negative way—scolding, criticizing, punishing. Sometimes he is so wrapped up in his job that he doesn't even know what's going on at school or in the home. Often his children will be rebellious when they reach adolescence. Some even become homosexuals; lacking an effective father figure, they over-identify with their mother.

These negative results don't have to happen, though. If the father is willing to grow, he can be a positive influence in the home. These men are usually unable to enjoy themselves unless they are working. But they can still make an effort to go on family picnics and interest themselves in their children's lives, even if it doesn't come easily. They are almost always good providers. Their economic view of life serves them well in the marketplace. But it doesn't work at home.

Wives can help by encouraging their husbands to interact with the family. All too frequently these women are willing to encourage their husbands indiscriminately; sometimes these men need to be reminded of the family's needs.

"I made a big mistake," Susan laments. "When our first child demanded me all the time, I accepted that and didn't encourage Tim to help with her. He was interested in his work and accepted the situation readily." She sighs. "Not that we're not happy. In fact, I feel certain that Tim is satisfied and content. But there's so much that I'd do differently if we were beginning over again."

Fathers need to instill their children with industriousness and a love of work. No fathers are better able to do this than these "economic" men. But it often requires them to devote a little less energy to their own careers, and a little more to the training of their children.

I know of one economic father who's been able to do this. John certainly deserves the label "go-getter." Since graduating from college, he's moved rapidly up the executive ladder in his company. But he still takes time to interact with his two children. He takes his son hunting and fishing, and he spends time working with them both on their homework and at various projects around the house. A somewhat impatient man, he is too critical of his children's performance at times. But by taking the time to cultivate their friendship, he's been able to provide a positive force in their development.

I know of several other well-functioning homes with this

sort of complementary relationship. The families work because the fathers make it work; they take time to be with their families. If they can also show love for their wives, the marriage can be rewarding, too. Their wives are usually very supportive, but their self-esteem can be damaged if they are treated as slaves. These men usually define human relationships in economic terms, but if they show appreciation for their wives' contribution, both partners will benefit from the marriage.

Independent Woman—Submissive Man

Of all the complementary marriages in this chapter, this one is the most likely to contain two unhappy spouses.

The pattern of interaction is set by the wife. She controls the relationship and manages the home. But this control doesn't make her satisfied or secure. She is a woman in conflict. She feels the need to be in control of things, but at the same time she wants a man she can look up to and respect. But she also fears aggressive men, so she settles for one she can control. This man's passivity often prevents him from achieving very much, and since his wife is an ambitious woman there is perpetual conflict.

We've often smiled—although it really isn't funny—at our friends Karen and Jack. A sincere Christian couple, they eventually sought help from a marriage counselor. After testing, they were told their personality types: Karen, independent and aggressive; Jack, submissive. Leaving the office after that session, Karen turned to Jack and said sternly, "Jack, you've just got to be more aggressive!"

The rest of the story is that with Jack's encouragement, once the girls were in school, Karen returned to school and got her master's degree, thus providing a channel for her energy. She then found a good job and is as happy as she can be. Jack, too, has learned to meet and relate better with people and to take on more responsibility at home. You might even call him quietly aggressive. As you might expect, their marriage has grown stronger.

The independent wife has other conflicts. She is unsure of her basic femininity. Often she comes from a family with problems that caused her to feel unloved. As a result, she fears being dependent on other people. She constantly proclaims her independence, bragging about any decision she makes and often lording it over her husband. By reveling in her independence, she tries to quell her own strong dependency needs.

The submissive husband has a different set of problems. As a child, he was probably deprived of his mother (often through death), although in some cases these men had very strong-willed mothers who beat them down. He needs a strong woman to take care of him, just as she needs a passive man who won't threaten her fragile self-concept.

Problems arise, however, because of her husband's unwillingness to shoulder responsibility and the wife's dissatisfaction. She chose this particular man because he would be easy to control. But she finds that bearing all the responsibility alone is no fun. And she makes it worse by undercutting any attempt he makes to assume leadership. When he asserts himself, she panics and puts him down. He quickly learns that the way to insure peace in the family is to give in.

There is a complementary balance to this relationship that often holds the family together. But neither spouse is happy.

This sort of marriage can work if the two are willing to grow. The wife must learn to control her fear of assertive men. In fact, she needs to encourage her husband in his decision-making attempts. The husband, on the other hand, must overcome his desire to be cared for as if he were a child. He must learn to take upon himself some of the child-care responsibilities. If she is willing to let his love and devotion (of which he probably has plenty) make her feel secure as a woman, and if he is willing to learn to assert himself as a man, with her support and strength to bolster him, the two can have an enjoyable, mutually satisfying marriage.

As always, the key is the willingness of the two to use their own strengths, appreciate those of the spouse, and learn to control their own weaknesses.

Seven

The Sexually Mature Woman

This chapter isn't entitled "The Sexually *Fulfilled* Woman" for a reason. The term "sexual fulfillment" has been used too often in the context of orgasms. The sexually fulfilled woman, we are told, is one who is able to have one or more orgasms every time she has sex with her husband. The woman who is unable to do so is not sexually fulfilled. Even in the Christian community we find books that say something along the lines of "any woman can have orgasms all the time."

But think what this can do to women who accept this sexual standard but fail to live up to it. Low self-esteem and feelings of inadequacy are only some of the possible results. Maggie—married twenty-five years—recently read one of these books. Her response was anger—"That is ridiculous"—and guilt—"Do you think Harry feels hurt that I don't have orgasms very often?"

Kathy Sue read some of these books before she married Richard. A virgin, she didn't know exactly what to expect, but all she'd read promised a fantastic physical sensation when she had an orgasm. Richard, also a virgin, was a tender and gentle (if a bit clumsy) lover, but Kathy Sue had some pain when Rich entered and no orgasm. Later, lying close to his bride, Rich whispered, "How was it, sweetheart?"

Tears sprang to her eyes. "It was fine."

Richard sensed her disappointment, but was too hurt to say anything. "Fine?" he thought. "Dinner was fine. The spring sunshine is fine. My lovemaking is supposed to be wonderful or great, but it's only *fine!*"

Most of the books have a good effect in dispelling some women's Victorian inhibitions about sexual expression. But I think they can do harm by placing too much emphasis on sexual fulfillment and orgasm. In the first place, they tend to take away from the spontaneous enjoyment of sex by introducing an element of pressure into marital lovemaking—pressure to have an orgasm.

"My husband has a mechanical mind anyway," Carole said sadly, "and he approaches sex the same way. He thinks if he pushes here and tickles me there, that I should automatically have an orgasm. It doesn't work." Her eyes flashed. "I'm too blamed honest to fake it, but he'd be happier if I did. I can see why women lie; there's so much pressure on them."

Secondly, the research simply doesn't support the claim that all women can experience orgasm every time if certain conditions are met. Female orgasms are sporadic; they depend upon biochemical and emotional factors independent of the wife's attitudes and her husband's techniques. Most women *can't* have an orgasm every time. But all women can enjoy sex.

A Source of Conflict About Sex

Over the last few years we've seen a strong attempt to deny that any innate sex differences exist. The sexes, we are told, are completely equal in all aspects; only socialization and discrimination make them different. In an earlier chapter, I discussed how wrong this belief is. But despite much scientific evidence to the contrary, it is still a popular idea.

Even some scientists have fostered the idea of sexual equality. The names "Masters and Johnson" have become well known over the last few years. Physician William

Masters and his psychologist wife Virginia Johnson have conducted much research on sexual intercourse. Most of it has had a valuable influence in clearing up questions and dispelling myths about sex. Unfortunately, Masters and Johnson fostered a few myths of their own. They conducted their research believing that men and women don't differ in sexual drive. In a book entitled *The Modernization of Sex,* Paul Robinson points out that although Masters and Johnson found many differences between their male and female subjects, they carefully downplayed these differences and called attention to the similarities.[1]

I suppose these scientists have good intentions when they insist that men and women are equal in every aspect. Perhaps they consider their orientation "fairer" than the one that insists upon innate sexual differences. Perhaps they fear that admitting sexual differences may make one sex feel inferior to the other.

Unfortunately, the opposite is true. Whenever truth is dethroned and a pleasant-sounding error is allowed to reign, the error always proves to be the harsher taskmaster. Women have suffered tremendously as a result of this new myth of sexual equality, partly because their very natures have been denied.

Lonnie Barbach, a sex therapist at the University of California Medical Center in San Francisco, describes the grief many women encounter as a result of the myth of sexual equality. She points out that expecting to have orgasms like men

> can lead to all sorts of erroneous conclusions. "Maybe it's not love" is one way of dismissing the difficulty. After all, you might feel that if it were really love, you would feel so turned on that you would naturally have orgasms. Because you don't have orgasms, you may assume that your partner must not be "Mr. Right," and you must not really be "in love" with him. Besides, if he really loved you, wouldn't he know how to "give" you an orgasm? Since he doesn't give you orgasms, you may conclude that he must not love you enough.[2]

Others have reported similar experiences. Feminist Margaret Rosoff wrote an interesting article in which she confessed that she had experienced years of frustration and unhappiness over her failure to have orgasms in view of the constant popular pressure saying that she should. Even Kinsey himself reported frequent examples of women who labeled themselves inferior and worthless because they couldn't have orgasms.

Yet, despite all this, the popular attitude prevails that women are no different from men in their capacity for sexual enjoyment. Despite her description of the psychological pain engendered by the sexual equality myth, Dr. Barbach, in her book *For Yourself: The Fulfillment of Female Sexuality,* attacks the "erroneous belief . . . that sex is not as necessary for women as it is for men."

Feminist Victoria Billings asserts that women should actually derive more pleasure from sex than men, since "it is woman, not man, who has an unlimited capacity for orgasm."

The sexually mature woman should derive much pleasure from sex, especially if she is married to a sexually mature man who understands her needs. But the statement that she should experience and enjoy it in the same way a man does is completely erroneous and ultimately harmful. Consider some of the results of research on sex differences in sexuality and sexual drive.

1. *Women consistently report less desire for sex than men do.* Marriages in which men report desire for more frequent intercourse outnumbers marriages in which the trend is reversed by more than two to one. I can't find a single study showing that married women in general desire intercourse more often than married men.

2. Despite the influence of the "sexual revolution," *women today have no more orgasms than women forty years ago.* It is believed that only slightly more than one fourth of women today have an orgasm every time they make love. Many report that they *never* have orgasms.[3]

3. *Women's inability to have orgasms cannot be related to poor techniques on the part of their husbands.* In fact,

one survey conducted by Dr. Anthony Pietropinto found that more than half of the men in his survey "were willing to go to any lengths to ensure their partner's satisfaction."[4] In one of the most thorough reviews of all the scientific information done on female orgasm, psychologist Seymour Fisher concluded:

> The notion that a woman's orgasm difficulties reflect her husband's poor love-making techniques . . . does not stand up well against the available research evidence. The extensive studies by Terman, in which wives and their husbands were evaluated in detail, turned up few, if any, consistent correlations between diverse husband attributes (including sexual behavior) and wife's orgastic ability. It is also true that Kinsey . . . and others have generally been unable to show that a woman's orgasm consistency is related to several different aspects of the husband's sexual behavior (for example, how long he persists in applying sexual stimulation to his wife). In the present writer's studies there were no consistent correlations between variables that certainly reflect the husband's sexual behavior (number of intercourse positions, amount of foreplay, and duration of sexual stimulation) and the wife's orgasm consistency.[5]

4. Some sex therapists report that *even with practice many women are unable to have orgasms*. In fact, intensive training *and* practice are not able to appreciably increase female orgasms. Fisher found that only one percent of the women studied were able to increase the number of orgasms, and only eight percent of the completely nonorgasmic women were able to have an occasional orgasm, with training and practice. However, Fisher also concluded that there was no indication that the women who failed to attain orgasms regularly were any more anxious, inhibited, or maladjusted than the women who achieved orgasms consistently.[6]

5. Evidence from many different cultures indicates that *women simply do not enjoy sex as much as men*. Even after years of sexual experience within marriage, a large number of women report that they do not get much satisfaction out

of sex with their husbands. One study of married couples found that ninety percent of the husbands found sex enjoyable, while only fifty-six percent of the wives did. These findings have held up, with some changes in statistics, in surveys done in the United States, England, Mexico, and Puerto Rico. The number of wives who give "very positive" statements about sex varies from a low of twenty percent to a high of about fifty percent. For men, the percentages remain consistently high across cultures.[7]

I think this difference in enjoyment is caused by the basic difference between men and women. Many women confide, "After we have a fight, my husband wants to make love to make up. But I don't want to do it until after we've made up."

Alice, trapped in an unhappy marriage with an abusive, unfaithful husband, said, "I can handle having sex with Larry—I hardly dare refuse him. But I won't kiss him. I don't want to touch him. He can use my body, but he can't have my mind."

The clincher to this story is that Larry told a counselor, "Sure, our sex life is fine. We do it three or four times a week."

Far too often, women shortchange themselves by never voicing their emotional needs, which have such a strong influence on their enjoyment of the physical act of sex.

Do lesbians enjoy sex more than their heterosexual sisters? For years, members of the homosexual community have asserted that lesbians are able to achieve orgasms much more frequently than heterosexual women. Supposedly, women's greater tenderness, gentleness, and knowledge of female anatomy make lesbian sex more enjoyable than heterosexual sex. Research has disproved this assertion. Rita Bass-Hass, for example, reports that lesbian sex is no more enjoyable for women, and leads to no more orgasms, than heterosexual sex.[8]

6. Finally, research strongly indicates that *differences between male and female sex drive are due to biological factors.* Many psychologists argue that differences in the strength of sex drive are due to learning and socialization.

In other words, women are *trained* to inhibit their sexual drive more than men.

This belief has not stood the test of scientific investigation. Even while they sleep, males work off excess sexual tension through "nocturnal emissions"—orgasms triggered by sex dreams. If women had an equally strong but inhibited sex drive, we'd expect them to work off the resulting sexual tension through similar "orgasmic dreams." But research indicates that during puberty, males have about 131 times as many nocturnal dreams with orgasms as females do.[9] These differences are even more meaningful when you consider that females reach puberty about a year and a half earlier than males. The fact is that many young women—especially those who have accepted the absolute of sex only within marriage—go through their whole teen years and young adulthood without being "awakened" sexually. Without social pressure to go to bed with their boyfriends, they do not feel a strong physical need either.

The tragedy of teen-age premarital sex is that the old saying still holds true: Boys give love to get sex, but girls give sex to get love.

In actuality, the male hormone testosterone is the source of sexual desire in both men *and* women. If a woman is injected with testosterone, she will experience an almost immediate desire for sexual intercourse.

Men and women have *both* male and female sex hormones circulating in their bodies, although in widely different amounts. The female adrenal glands produce a small amount of testosterone, which is the source of women's sexual arousal. In fact, women who have their adrenal glands surgically removed will undergo a decrease in sexual desire. On the other hand, if a woman loses her feminine hormones (estrogen) she will not lose her sex drive. Testosterone is the key to sexual desire in both men and women. And since the male body produces about ten times as much testosterone as the female body, it follows that the two would have different levels of sexual desire and drive.

Women, with their lower level of sexual arousal, add an element of restraint to a drive that constantly attempts to defy control. If men had the same level of sexual arousal as women, there would probably be less sexual enjoyment all around. But if women had the same level of sexual arousal as men, we would live in a world that resembles dry lumber in a lightning storm. Sex would dominate us even more than it does now. Women act as a source of control over sexual activity through their greater ability to live without it and through their need to keep sex and love closely connected.

If you want to understand what women add to the sexual relationship, consider what takes place in the world of sex between men. Many studies have been done on the typical sex life of male homosexuals. These studies show a seamy, sordid picture of short, detached sexual experiences and wild promiscuity.

Two social scientists recently reported the results of in-depth interviews with almost one thousand homosexuals in the San Francisco Bay area. They found that homosexual men were much more promiscuous in their sexual relationships than heterosexual men. Almost half of the homosexuals interviewed reported that they had had over five hundred different lovers; almost thirty percent had had over one thousand sexual contacts, many of them with virtual strangers.[10] The fact that these men were from an area that has been very tolerant of homosexuals would argue against the theory that they were forced into this promiscuity by cultural hostility. Rather, this would seem to be the pattern of male-male relationships.

Woman's Sexual Nature

Several years ago, a new sexual practice started in California and then spread to other parts of the country. It was called "swinging" or "mate-swapping," and some social scientists predicted it would soon be practiced by the majority of American couples. Several influential people greeted the new "open marriage" as the wave of the future—a way to restore excitement to the sex act and rid couples of "sexual jealousy."

Fortunately, these predictions never panned out. Swinging never really caught on, despite much publicity. Today it is practiced by a very small (and shrinking) number of people. Who do we have to thank for the death of swinging? Research suggests that swinging is dying primarily because not enough women have supported it. Among couples who experimented with mate-swapping, studies show that the wives were almost always the ones who forced the couple to abandon it.[11]

All the knowledge we've gathered about sex indicates that for women the focus of attention is not upon the sex act itself, but upon the relationship it occurs within. Based upon a massive survey of female sexuality, Shere Hite concluded that "women liked sex more for feelings involved than for the purely physical sensations of intercourse per se."[12]

Even Masters and Johnson recognized the female need for a loving relationship, although they continued to downplay sex differences in their writings. In the treatment program they devised for sexual disorders, male clients would be supplied with a sex partner. But they asked their women clients to bring their own sex partners, because they knew from experience that men could easily accept sex without love; women couldn't.

Many other studies have found that for women to participate enthusiastically in sex, they must be satisfied with the quality of the marital relationship. One cross-cultural study conducted by Lee Rainwater found that wives in four different countries reported the same thing about sex: the more satisfying the emotional relationship, the more satisfying the sexual relationship. In fact, he found that wives in emotionally dissatisfying relationships actually picked fights with their husbands to avoid sexual intercourse. This supports other studies that show that wives' sexual responsiveness *decreases* as marital strife *increases*.

By their very nature, women bring a certain element of individuality and intimacy to the sexual relationship. A woman doesn't usually want sex for its own sake; she wants sex with a particular man. Through her, the sex act is not simply a mechanical release of tension and experience of pleasure; it is an affirmation of the love and commitment between two specific people. By being so intimately tied to a particular person, a woman's sex life reaffirms the importance and uniqueness of each partner.

This doesn't mean that every sex act must be preceded by hours of preparation—soft light, music, romance, and love talk. That type of sex should be present in a healthy sexual relationship, but every lovemaking session need not fit this pattern. If the overall relationship is filled with love and tenderness, most women will cherish the occasional passionate, spontaneous act of sexual intercourse that men enjoy so much. For the sexually mature and loving couple, there is room for a variety of types of lovemaking—from the planned, romantic time at a quiet motel to the quick, spontaneous act of love while the children are napping.

This should not imply that all men are animals, looking for every possible opportunity to take advantage of unwilling women. More and more, today's man realizes that his woman has emotional as well as physical needs. Good, enjoyable, satisfying sex doesn't begin at bedtime. It begins with a cheerful husband at breakfast, perhaps a call home during the day, and a hand with the children in the evening. The couple's mutual love and respect is what makes lovemaking special.

Christian men have always been taught to uphold fidelity and to love their wives, but this doesn't change the fact that man's sexual nature differs from woman's. The sexually mature husband and wife are able to recognize and accept these differences, making adjustments first to one nature and then to the other.

Don and Kira's marital problems were deeply rooted in Don's dependence upon his mother and his inability to relate to his wife. Kira keenly felt his lack of attention, his dissatisfaction with her cooking, her housecleaning, with everything she did. Sex became reduced to Don's "let's-do-it-and-get-it-over-with" attitude, and Kira despaired of pleasing him in bed. One night she showered, carefully combed her hair, and put on her makeup. Then, wearing nothing but Chanel Number Five, she crept into the living room where Don was watching TV and sat on his lap.

"Not now, Kira," he snapped, pushing her aside.

Don was totally out of tune to Kira's needs, and their marriage was in graver danger than either of them suspected.

Paul and Kim had a different problem. Paul was a day person, and Kim didn't wake up until around nine at night. They never seemed to go to bed at the same time. So they compromised. Kim came to bed just to make love, often getting up afterwards to sew or write letters. And sometimes Paul woke her for a quick bit of loving before he went to work. The compromise worked well.

As each couple finds their own unique rhythm for lovemaking, their relationship will be enriched beyond that which is possible if one demands and the other merely complies.

Woman's Sexual Response

Genuine affection, love, tenderness, and other such qualities are necessary to a woman's sexual response. In fact, if these are present most women will enjoy sex even without orgasm. Many women find much pleasure just in giving their husbands pleasure.

Besides the quality of the marital relationship, several other important factors determine whether or not a woman will experience full sexual satisfaction, with orgasm.

In the first place, the quality of a woman's early relationship with her own father plays a strong role in her later sexual experiences. In his extensive study of the female orgasm, Seymour Fisher found that in order to reach a climax, women must feel that their husbands can be trusted to stay with them.[13] Whether or not a woman feels this way is strongly dependent on the quality of her relationship with her father. If that relationship was filled with trust, love, and affection—if a girl felt she could always approach her father without being rejected—then she is better prepared to enjoy full sexual satisfaction with her husband. That is not to say that a woman who had a poor relationship with her father cannot have a good marriage, but it may be more difficult. If both partners take this into consideration, they have a better chance of success.

Several years ago, a couple of studies on the sexual experience of Christian women revealed they had more orgasms than non-Christian women.[14] This came as a shock to those who consider Christians outdated, straight-laced individuals whose God-imposed restrictions take the joy out of life. But in light of the "trust" factor mentioned above, these findings should have come as no surprise. Orgasms are not the result of precision sexual mechanics, but a by-product of the love and trust two people have for each other. If women need to trust their husbands in order to have orgasms, then what more reasonable place to find trust than in Christian familes? Fathers are more likely to be present, and to be involved with their children, since Christians have always been taught to look upon marriage as forever, and upon family responsibilities as primary.

A second influence upon a woman's sexual satisfaction is her own attitude. Some very conscientious Christian women are convinced that personal enjoyment of any kind is a sin. This is less true today than it has been in the past, but it is still an impediment to sexual fulfillment for some Christian women.

This belief is a throwback to the ancient heresy that all material things—including our bodies—are evil. Hildy never knew she was supposed to enjoy sex. And for the first few years of marriage, she didn't. Actually, her feelings toward it were more neutral than anything else. But as her love for Carl grew and deepened, and she felt important to him and her daughter, she began to desire his lovemaking. And she was almost frightened.

"Sex is a gift from God," a friend commented one day. Hildy pondered that offhand remark, and gradually her love for Carl began to overcome her inhibitions. The first time she actively participated in lovemaking, Carl was shocked.

"Hildy, that was wonderful! We ought to go off by ourselves for a weekend." Hildy blushed like a bride.

Other women may be forced into a sort of anxious concern by the circumstances they live in. Housework and children often pull a woman's attention away from the joys of lovemaking. Some women find it extremely difficult to have orgasms when they make love in the same place they work. But these same women can be very orgasmic when taken to a romantic, get-away-from-it-all location. It's a wise husband who takes his wife on an occasional rendezvous away from home. Such a change of scenery allows a woman to feel romantic and to devote her full attention to the act of love.

These and many other factors—some physiological—make women much less likely to achieve orgasm than men. In fact, research indicates that a significant number of women will not have orgasms at all. But that shouldn't be a reason for despair, low self-esteem, or frustration. Scientific research just doesn't support the idea that any woman can have orgasms on a regular basis. In fact, this sentiment can make sex a very anxious task for the couple who define the success of their sex life by whether or not the woman has an orgasm. Pressure to succeed has no place in the bedroom.

After all the manuals have been read and the books perused, sexual enjoyment all boils down to the personal qualities of the individual husband and wife—their willingness to talk and to listen to one another, their capacity to overcome embarrassment and to experiment freely and spontaneously, their sensitivity to one another's needs and desires, and their ability to accept one another and themselves.

As I see it, these personal qualities are more important than the specific techniques the couple uses. The best lovemaking takes place when a certain romantic excitement fills the air. This type of excitement is not fostered by technique.

The sexually mature man is certainly willing to use those

techniques that his wife finds enjoyable. He is willing to be romantic, to take his time and let the excitement build up slowly, to learn to stimulate and caress his wife's body in all the right places, and to express his love for her often. The sexually mature woman is able to give herself unreservedly to her husband and to readily respond to his initiations. But she is also able to accept her sexual nature and the attraction it holds for her husband, whether she is orgasmic or not.

Eight

The Energetic Woman

About two years ago I began collecting information on the topic of energy. Part of the data was published in a book entitled *The Energy and Vitality Book*.[1] Since that time I've continued to study such questions as "What determines energy level?" and "How can energy output be increased?"

A three-page questionnaire I've constructed asks people various questions about their energy level. So far more than two hundred people have filled out the questionnaire, and their responses have yielded some very interesting findings.

One is that energy level is related to self-esteem. In other words, people who say they have a high level of energy also tend to report a high level of self-esteem. Conversely, those who say their energy level is low also indicate that their self-esteem is low. And the two seem to feed off one another; as one increases, the other tends to increase as well.

A second finding is that women tend to report more energy problems than men. Although the answers vary a great deal from one woman to the next, the women in the survey more often reported swings in energy level, difficulty organizing their work, lower levels of productivity, and a greater need for more energy than men did.

These findings have implications for women's self-esteem. If our perceived energy level is closely tied in with how we feel about ourselves, then one way to develop a more positive self-image is to increase our level of energy.

Sources of Female Energy Problems

Before offering suggestions for increasing energy output, I'd like to consider some of the reasons why women may have more problems with energy than men. At least four factors affect a woman's energy level.

1. *The menstrual cycle.* A significant number of women (thirty percent, according to some surveys) report severe discomfort and dysphoria (feeling unwell) associated with their menstrual periods. An even larger percentage experience a drop in self-confidence and productivity during the four or five days prior to the menstrual period.

This is called the "premenstrual syndrome," and it affects a woman's energy level and productivity. Psychologist Katherine Dalton found that test scores and grades drop among schoolgirls during the premenstrual part of the cycle.[2] Others have found that accidents, crime, suicide, and psychiatric problems increase during this period. The implications are that a very basic type of energy—the energy to cope—is lowered.

For many years, psychologists (mostly males) believed such symptoms were "all in a woman's head." Even today, despite much evidence to the contrary, some professionals and laymen hold the same view. But premenstrual symptoms are very real; they are a natural result of rises and drops in the output of female hormones, particularly estrogen and progesterone.

One study explored the effects of two types of birth control pills upon menstrual cycle symptoms. The first type allowed the female hormones to rise and fall in their usual manner. The second type maintained the hormones at a high level throughout the cycle. Women who took the first type of birth control pill continued to show physical and emotional fluctuations. But women who took the second type showed no mood swings or physical changes over the menstrual cycle. Since none of the women in the study were told how the pills would affect their hormone levels, it's hard to attribute the results to something "in their heads."[3]

The rise and fall of hormones associated with the menstrual cycle no doubt affects a woman's energy level, as well as her feelings about herself. Perhaps this explains why women more often than men answered "mood swings" to the question, "What are the major factors affecting your energy level?"

2. *The impact of children.* There's no doubt that full-time childrearing involves demands rarely found in other jobs. Patience, conscientiousness, and self-control are sometimes taxed to their limits by children who themselves have abundant wellsprings of energy. Since they often lack the resources to channel that energy, their emotions sometimes explode freely upon their caretakers, like waves beating upon a rock. Over time, the rock can weaken; the waves never do.

Grappling with children while they learn to control themselves can be a sure energy drainer. What's more, the positive effects of good childrearing may not show up for years and years. This is an important source of frustration for many conscientious Christian mothers, yet husbands and fathers rarely appreciate it. Women who devote themselves fully to the character training of their children, as many Christian mothers do, involve themselves in a task that has eternal repercussions. Yet despite its crucial importance, mothers don't get immediate feedback when they do a good job.

Added to the problems mothers normally face is the fact that homemaking and motherhood have come under strong ideological attack from people who see that role as demeaning and stifling. These messages can easily discourage women who devote their full attention to childrearing. Optimism and enthusiasm about one's life-work (important energy-stimulators) can easily be lost under the new ideological assaults.

Finally, mothers can feel energy-depleted due to problems with very difficult children. Some children are harder to train (and harder to live with) because they are either strong-willed, emotional, or very demanding. Psychiatrists Alexander Thomas and Stella Chess began a study in the early 1960s that made several interesting revelations about the effects some children have upon their parents, and in particular upon their mothers. Psychologists have traditionally asserted that the child's entire personality is molded by the parents, and they've consequently been quick to blame mothers for children's personality problems. But Thomas and Chess found that children enter the world with their own personalities, and that the mother's guilt and despair are frequently a reaction to a difficult temperament.[4]

I've noticed that many women who feel very satisfied with their role as mothers have a strong interest in building the characters and developing the spiritual lives of their children. These women seem immune to the various outside assaults upon their role. They see their job as more than a caretaker. As a result, they don't suffer from the energy stagnation that affects some mothers.

3. *Social needs.* As mentioned earlier, writer Maggie Scarf's recent book attempted to answer the question, "Why do women experience depressions so much more often than men?" (as much as six times as often, according to some studies). Mrs. Scarf spent many hours in mental clinics conducting lengthy interviews with women undergoing depressions. She also marshalled an array of statistical data that reinforced the conclusions she had drawn from those interviews and observations. Depression among women, she states, "has reached 'epidemic proportions.' " And contrary to popular opinion, it occurs as often among highly successful career women as among full-time homemakers. In fact, it strikes women of all classes and life situations, without discrimination.

Why this alarming increase in depression and dysphoria? Mrs. Scarf concluded that women are vulnerable because of their greater need for stable social relations. The breakup of the family unit, she states, along with the instability in relationships associated with a highly mobile society, have left women depleted and depressed. Men can more easily shift from one relationship to another. Women, on the other hand, need stability in their relationships.

It doesn't take a Ph.D. in psychology to realize that depression inhibits a person's energy level. Anyone who has watched a person who feels depressed has observed slowed movements, lack of motivation, and an absence of interest in life.

These statistics provide further evidence that a woman's lot is more closely tied in with the family than is man's (although both are highly dependent upon a stable family system). If women are to enjoy their full potential of energy output, they must live in a world where family relationships and commitments can be counted on.

4. *Differences in sexual and aggressive drives.* Some psychologists differentiate between two sources or levels of energy. The first is the most basic. It probably flows from the action of the cells, from their synthesis of glucose and their electrical activity. The second source is more peripheral, involving emotional, sexual, and aggressive drives.

Research indicates that men and women probably do not differ in their level of emotional energy, but men do have stronger sexual and aggressive drives. These drives provide a source of energy that can be drawn upon when extra effort is needed.

Unlocking Latent Energy

The fact that men have stronger sexual and aggressive drives does not mean that they win the energy contest hands down. We can actually talk in terms of two types of energy: long-term and short-term. Long-term energy is the ability to maintain one's health and viability over an extended period of time. It involves living a long, healthy life. Short-term energy, on the other hand, refers to immediate stamina and endurance. A person with excellent short-term energy might live a very short life. In fact, too much short-term energy may lessen one's long-term energy by "burning the candle at both ends."

Apparently, this is true of men and women. Women usually live longer than men, and they are less susceptible to many of the diseases that afflict men. In the past, psychologists have explained away this observation by saying that the strain of working to support a family shortens men's lives. This observation is no longer considered valid. Females generally outlive males among all mammals. And even in those cultures where women work harder than men, they still outlive men.

Women *do* have more long-term energy than men. It's mainly in the area of short-term energy that women are likely to experience problems. So I'd like to offer the following suggestions to help women unlock latent energy, increase productivity, improve work habits, and conquer the conditions that drain energy.

1. *Set aside time to recuperate.* Every woman (and man) needs time alone—time to "recharge the batteries" and allow new energy to flow in. How much time alone is needed will vary quite a bit from one person to the next. Some need recuperation time every day. Others can get by on once-a-week sessions. But everyone needs these periods.

Many of us are inclined to feel guilty about stealing time alone, especially those of us who take the work ethic very seriously. But we should remember that our Lord set aside time alone to meditate and pray, and He advised His disciples to do the same. His responsibilities were heavy; the salvation of the world was upon His shoulders. And yet He alternated between the mountain and the multitude. Energy, alertness, and peace of mind were important for the successful completion of His mission, and they are important for ours as well.

Christ is our example, in this as in all other aspects of living. His rest was not self-indulgent. Prayer and meditation constituted a large portion of His time alone.

Recuperation sessions are very important for mothers of

small children. Since mothering is not just a nine-to-five activity, it's easy to fall into the trap of constant laboring. But mothers need time alone as much as anyone (probably more!). One young mother said to me, "I like to take an hour-long bath in the early part of the evening. My husband watches the kids while I bathe. If I couldn't have this time to myself, I don't think I'd be able to cope with all the work I have to do."

2. *Use the energizing power of inspiration.* We tend to believe that a low energy level is due to physical tiredness. In other words, when we feel listless, unmotivated, or unenthusiastic, we often attribute it to a lack of physical energy.

But many of our energy problems today are due to mental, not physical, fatigue. The mind is as much a source of energy as the body (possibly more so). That's why people who seem to have an abundant source of energy are usually those who also have a very positive and healthy mental outlook. Their optimism and enthusiasm insure a constant flow of energy.

So your mind, not necessarily your body, is the key to your energy problems. Do you feel tired, depleted, listless? Check your thinking. The chances are good that your thought pattern has become negative and defeatist.

It's easy to fall into a negative thinking pattern, with all the pressures and fears that impinge upon us daily. Big city noises lower our resistance. The state of the economy and the possibility of nuclear war intimidate us. The breakdown of the family and the separation of friends and mates make us pessimistic and anxious. Add to all this the minor irritations that come with children, mates, and work, and you have a prescription for negative thinking.

Whenever negative emotions or thinking patterns eat away at our energy, we need a burst of inspiration. There's nothing like a shot of inspiration to free our dormant energy and make us feel alive and enthusiastic again.

I strongly recommend that you reserve a section of your bookshelf for inspirational literature. Books that promote positive attitudes, for instance, can inspire and counter negative thought patterns. Biographies of missionaries, innovators, or people who have overcome great odds are often interesting and inspiring. It's hard to feel listless and unmotivated after reading such literature.

I find that a brief inspirational session early in the morning unlocks enough energy to last all day. These sessions are especially important when you have to face a difficult task for which you have little self-confidence. One man used this technique whenever he had to give a public speech. Although he dreaded speaking, the inspiration sessions filled him with such confidence and optimism that he always performed successfully.

Try this method whenever you feel energy-depleted. I guarantee that you will feel a surge of energy and enthusiasm. And while you're filling your bookcase with these books, don't neglect the most inspiring book of all—the Bible. There's a power in those words of Scripture, a power that has energized men and women for the last two millennia. Daily Bible study is a must for the woman who wants to use her energy creatively and productively. As Christ said to His disciples: ". . . the words that I speak unto you, they are spirit, and they are life" (John 6:63).

3. *Think small.* This runs against the grain of much popular writing, which advocates thinking big. But the ability to think small—to break up work into small "chunks" or units—is one of the best ways to overcome procrastination and insure that you have enough energy and motivation to complete any task, no matter how large and intimidating.

Writing is one of my most difficult tasks. I stare at an empty notebook and realize that I must fill it (and many others) with my own ideas. What if those ideas never come? Added to that, the thought that I must sit down to write an entire book is very frightening. It has made procrastination a constant opponent—defeated one time only to arise another. I have wasted much time and energy just fighting myself.

While battling this enemy of procrastination, I came upon a method that has made working on any task, including writing, much easier for me. The real enemy was my own thinking—I was thinking too big. I was thinking in terms of writing an entire book when I could not possibly write an entire book in one sitting.

I decided to break the task down, to narrow my thinking. First I thought in terms of writing one chapter only, but even that was too much. So I narrowed it to a page, then to a paragraph, and then to the smallest possible unit I knew I could complete successfully—a single sentence. I decided that whenever I got ready to write, I would not think beyond one single sentence.

After all, I couldn't write more than one sentence at a time, so why think beyond it? The thought of writing a book inhibited my energy, but the thought of writing only a single sentence actually exhilarated me. Enthusiasm was aroused; energy flowed outward; interest perked up. And since adopting this method, I've been able to do a tremendous amount of writing—more than I ever could have accomplished without it.

This same method will work just as well with other types of work. The trick is to break it down into the smallest possible unit that you can complete successfully at one time, and then refuse to think beyond that unit. If you hate to wash dishes, then plan to wash only one dish. If you are a student who hates to study, then plan to read only one page of a dreaded textbook a day (or break it down to one paragraph, if it's an especially difficult textbook). Refuse to think beyond the one small unit. You know you can successfully complete that one unit, so you will feel good about yourself as you work. And that good feeling will reward you in a way that will make the work much easier in the future.

You won't feel as good about yourself if you think in terms of reading the entire book, because you can't possibly complete that large task at one sitting. And thinking in terms of huge tasks makes it easier to procrastinate or to avoid the task altogether. Thinking in terms of small units makes it easy to work. Who couldn't read one page, or wash one dish, or write one sentence? You're almost guaranteed success!

Right now you're probably thinking, "If I write no more

than one sentence a day or read no more than one page a day, it will take me forever to complete the task.'' That would be true if you actually did no more than the one small unit per day. But once you get into the task, momentum will take over and you will actually be able to work with enthusiasm. The main function of the one-small-unit method is getting you started.

This is true of my writing efforts. To me, the most difficult times are at the beginning and the end of the writing task. At the beginning it's hard to get started, and at the end it's easy to feel depleted and sick of the whole thing. In the middle, momentum takes over and I actually look forward to writing. It's mainly at the beginning and the end of a project that I rely heavily on the one-small-unit approach.

This method works very well for most people, according to the feedback I've received. It's an excellent method for overcoming procrastination and for encouraging efficient use of time. Harriet Beecher Stowe wrote *Uncle Tom's Cabin* during snatches of time between household duties, and Longfellow translated the *Inferno* during the ten-minute period each day that he waited for his coffee to boil.

Try this method for yourself. It's an excellent way to keep your energy flowing into productive work and to feel constantly enthusiastic about your efforts.

4. *Make use of the energizing power of interest.* One of the most effective energy stimulators available is strong interest. People who are genuinely interested in what they are doing always seem to have energy to throw behind their tasks. On the other hand, people who are uninterested seem to have little energy.

When you go to a store, you can tell very quickly if the salesperson is really interested in his job. Nothing is more unimpressive than a salesperson who acts as if waiting on customers is the equivalent of a life sentence in Siberia. Their lack of interest usually expresses itself in a listless, apathetic demeanor. The truly interested salesperson is the one who seems energetic and involved, and whose enthusiasm makes you more enthusiastic.

My wife and I have a friend who has a variety of strong

interests. She is into photography, macrame, and other hobbies. Her enthusiasm seems to generate a constant source of energy to throw into these activities. She is also interested in *everything* she does and every person she talks to. She commits herself fully—both mind and body—to whatever task she undertakes, treating each one as if it were glamorous and exciting. And she never seems to want for energy.

I think one of the secrets of maintaining an interest in all tasks is to commit ourselves fully to that task. All too often we undertake our duties (and sometimes our hobbies) with one foot on the throttle and the other on the brake. We aren't really sure the task is that rewarding.

Very young children rarely suffer from that affliction. They're interested in everything. Every new object is a source of wonder and amazement. They will spend time studying a kitchen pan or trying on their mother's shoes. Their strong interest in the world elicits an unceasing flow of energy. Even when their bodies begin to demand rest, they will fight off sleep with a bitter intensity, refusing to depart from their fascinating world.

We adults, on the other hand, welcome bedtime as a release from our drab, uninteresting lives. After all, we've seen it all and done it all hundreds of times. And yet, if we wish to be truly energetic people we must also be intensely interested people.

Few jobs are without boredom or repetition. Even actors and actresses, who most of us believe have a glamorous profession, must spend most of their time learning and reciting over and over again the scripts that are essential to their jobs. They also spend much time waiting—in their dressing rooms for their next scene or in the makeup room preparing for their part.

The energetic woman is able to maintain her interest even in the face of repetition. Sometimes that requires thinking about the ultimate goal rather than the repetitive activities that lead to that goal. Sometimes it means making subtle changes in the way you perform your activities. And sometimes it involves cultivating an interest and enthusiasm about life itself, and about all the fascinating things around us. Being mature does not mean we shed everything about ourselves that is childlike. That childlike interest in and enthusiasm about the world is a key to energy itself.

5. *Learn to handle your mood swings.* Most people, I'm sure, realize that mood is related to energy level. If your mood is high, your energy level, self-esteem, interest, and enthusiasm will also be high. But when your mood drops, all these attributes drop along with it. Thus, handling mood swings is an important part of becoming a more energetic person.

Two completely different strategies exist for dealing with mood swings. The first is to *adjust your activities to the mood swing* rather than trying to change it. This strategy has the advantage of emphasizing self-acceptance. Since many mood swings are the result of biochemical changes, why fight the mood change or condemn yourself for having it? Why not simply accept it as a fact of life, adjust your schedule to it, and continue on about your business? In other words, why waste energy fighting biology?

One young woman went after her most active goals while she was experiencing the high part of her mood swings. During that time, she would write lengthy novels, clean her house thoroughly, and pursue projects that required a strong activity level. When the lows came, she would turn to more "passive" activities such as reading, reflecting on problems, and planning for the future.

The second strategy is to *work at changing the mood swing.* This approach gives less emphasis to the biochemical factors in mood swings; instead, it accentuates the changes in thinking that accompany those swings.

According to this approach, even if biochemical factors *cause* the mood swing, thoughts and actions still have a strong influence. Some people make their mood swings worse by indulging in a negative string of thoughts. So the way to handle a low mood is to practice thinking positive thoughts and performing positive actions.

Neurological studies do suggest that an innate "feedback system" exists between our facial muscles and our neuronal system. If the facial muscles contract downward into a frown, certain neurons that control mood are activated to bring the emotions into balance with the posture. Consequently, a person's mood drops when he frowns. The implications are that thought and action patterns do play a strong role in mood swings.

Which method should you adopt? That probably depends upon your situation and the cause of your mood swing. Most likely, both strategies should be adopted to one degree or another. Experiment with each to find which combination works best for you.

As for the practical question of how to best utilize the two methods, I have several suggestions, whether you decide to adjust to the mood swing or try to change it.

1. *As much as possible, keep your attention off yourself.* When mood drops, there is a strong temptation to brood about past hurts, bad experiences, and personal failings. Try to avoid these thoughts. They only weaken self-esteem. And they can turn a minor mood swing into a serious depression.

2. *Try to engage in some deliberate positive thinking.* That's not what you *feel* like doing. You want to think about despair and doom. But resist the temptation. Now is the time to pull out some inspirational literature and soak it up. I find it greatly beneficial to set aside time every morning, when my mood is low, to read some inspirational thoughts. It prevents me from giving in to depression, and it checks the stream of negative thoughts that always lurk behind a downswing in mood.

3. *Avoid defeatist posture.* Make a conscious effort to sit up straight, to get out of a chair quickly, to hold your head high, and to smile. If you can act confidently and energetically in these little areas, true feelings of confidence and energy will soon follow.

4. *Breathe deeply and smoothly.* When mood drops, there is a temptation to breathe shallowly and haltingly. The resulting deprivation of oxygen aggravates the drop in mood. One of the quickest ways to reestablish energy and resolve is to force yourself to take deep, full breaths.

5. *Accept yourself as you are, even with the mood swings.* You can't avoid all swings in mood. Even the prophet Elijah couldn't. Don't look upon it as punishment from God or as an opportunity to punish yourself. Chances are, it's a simple biochemical event. It will pass.

6. *Make use of the privilege of prayer.* Few experiences can fill us with energy, hope, optimism, and joy as prayer can. Christ prayed often, sometimes choosing prayer over sleep. We miss a vital opportunity to connect ourselves with the Source of all energy when we don't pray.

God's Spirit is the most powerful force available to man. He can sweep away guilt, despair, dejection, and all the other energy depleters in just a few seconds. He can fill us with love, hope, and optimism; He can inspire us; and He can unlock our most potent reserves of energy.

Every woman (and man) should set aside time each day to be alone with God—to pour out her fears, hopes, desires, and needs, and to be healed of sin and despair. This daily experience with God energizes in the most beneficial way— with the power of love.

Nine

The Stages
in a Woman's Life

A friend of mine has several children, each of whom could only be described as "difficult." They vary in age from about two to eight, and each is able to get into the maximum amount of trouble possible for that particular age group. Their mother, a very easygoing woman, explains instances of misbehavior by saying, "That's just a stage he [or she] is going through." Her "stages" are defined in terms of misbehavior—"The stage of screaming and yelling," the "stage of pulling the cat's tail," the "stage of sassing the teacher," and on and on.

We might chuckle at this attempt to blame "stages of development" for lax discipline. But definite stages in the lives of all human beings *can* be identified, and research strongly suggests that how successfully a person handles himself at each stage determines his future self-esteem, personality, and character.

As mentioned in the second chapter, women's lives are more sharply divided into stages than are men's lives. Menstruation brings with it an abrupt change in physiology; marriage usually changes a woman's role very quickly; children bring about even greater changes in women's lives; and menopause also carries with it a sharp biological and psychological shift. How a woman handles herself during these stages determines much of her later happiness and self-esteem. In part, self-esteem is a cumulative experi-

129

ence: It changes over the years. And one of the best ways to assess the impact of this accumulation of changes is to divide the typical woman's life into stages.

The best discussion of the stages of human development probably was presented by psychologist Erik Erikson. In the remainder of this chapter, we will look at Erikson's description of human development, with one extra stage thrown in—the prenatal. We will concentrate on the factors that affect a woman's self-concept and look at some differences in the natures and experiences of males and females at each stage.

The Prenatal Stage

Several centuries ago, a philosopher speculated that if we could glimpse into the pregnant womb we'd probably find that what happens during the first nine months of life is much more interesting than what takes place during the remaining seventy years.

This statement is somewhat extreme. But the knowledge we've acquired about prenatal development does reveal a fascinating stage in human growth.

For the first six weeks after conception, boy and girl babies are almost indistinguishable from one another. Then, around the seventh week after conception, as the heart and blood vessels ripen, a boy's sex organs begin producing male hormones. Those hormones are then carried through the bloodstream into the brain. Once there, like an army of construction workers, these hormones begin the job of forming the brain into the "masculine" pattern.

For girls, the process is slightly different. Since no male hormones are present during this early stage, the brain continues to develop into the female pattern. Thus, a female brain will develop unless something is added to the process—the male hormones. They must be added during this critical period between the seventh and tenth weeks after conception. After this time, no hormones can affect the brain in relation to sex determination. The baby, then, is irrevocably male or female.

This is one of the most important recent discoveries in the field of biology: that the brains of men and women are different (with individual variations, of course). It has tremendous implications for the way men and women grow up, for the kinds of experiences and problems each is likely to have, and for the strategies each is likely to use in resolving their problems. In other words, this research confirms what poets and philosophers have long recognized: Men and women are not only built differently; they also think differently.

The male brain produces traits we usually call aggressiveness, initiative, dominance, and authority. The female brain is associated with such attributes as nurturance, empathy, an orientation toward children, and a concern for the welfare of the small group. This does not mean that men have no nurturing qualities or that women have no initiative. Both men and women have characteristics in both categories, but strong sex differences do exist in these areas.

One obvious result of these differences is that males are more likely to get into trouble than females. Even at two or three, little boys are more likely to whack a friend over the head with a truck or saw the handles off your mop and broom. Little girls require less policing during the school years, too. Because girls mature faster than boys, often the six-year-old boy just isn't physically mature enough for school. He can't sit still. He wiggles and fidgets, and his attention span isn't as long as that of his six-year-old girl classmates. I always wondered why so many little boys have poor handwriting and are notoriously poorer readers than are girls. Then I learned that many girls start school with an edge of maturity over their same-age brothers.

The greater male aggressiveness and initiative is no doubt a major reason why boys find it easier to break the ties with home and family than girls do. The old saying, "A son's a son 'til he takes him a wife, but a daughter's a daughter for the rest of her life," has much support from psychological research. Even in adulthood, women are more likely than men to maintain close ties with parents.

This intense involvement of women with their parents, especially with their mothers, has obvious advantages. It holds the extended family together, even through lengthy separations over long distances. Women are often the ones who write letters and remember birthdays and holidays.

But if family relationships are conflictive, or if the parents are overbearing and domineering, women often suffer more than men. Several books have been written lately on the topic of mother/daughter conflicts. All seem to point to a psychological dependence of women upon their mothers. And if the mother can't let go, some women may have problems with their mothers even into late adulthood.

Sixty-year-old Madge is still unable to express a thought of her own without her seventy-eight-year old mother correcting or disagreeing. Mother demands that Madge call her morning, noon, and night. This is not a case of a helpless mother who needs a daughter's care, but of a selfish woman who has refused to let her daughter grow up. When Madge makes any break toward independence, Mother becomes "deathly ill" with a headache, stomach pains, or both.

Another result of these differences between male and female brains has to do with sex roles. The female brain is predisposed to acquire such traits as empathy and the desire to nurture, which means that women are generally more closely involved with childrearing. Men, on the other hand, are programmed to acquire most of the leadership positions within society and to be seen as the main authority figures in the home. In fact, this is the pattern that prevails in all cultures. (There has been much debate about the existence of matriarchy [not to be confused with matrilineal], but not one such culture has been found. See my book *Sex Roles and the Christian Family* for a more complete discussion.)

Now, most Christian women have no trouble accepting this fact of sex differences. To them, husbandly leadership is a blessing. But to others, it has become a sign of oppression.

Part of this resentment is due to the fact that a number of men have misused their leadership role to make unreasonable demands upon their wives. Too many wives have been made unhappy under the guise of "superiority"—supposedly given to their husbands by God Himself!

Men have a certain power, certain *rights*. But they have certain *responsibilities* as well. One male marriage counselor believes men should be first: the first to apologize, the first to get up on winter mornings to light the fires, and so on.

Emily was dissatisfied with her role as a Christian wife. She felt that her husband had power she didn't have, and she resented him for it. Somehow she could not see the great power she wielded in the home. She had the ability to make her home heaven or hell for her husband and children. Her cheerful energy could have transformed their house into a palace, where the family loved to gather and bring friends. Instead, both husband and children avoided home and churlish, complaining Emily.

This resentment is very destructive to families and to the happiness of women caught up in it. We all need to feel we are growing and progressing, but we also need to accept biological realities. One set of traits is neither superior nor inferior to the other. Only by accepting these differences will we be able to accept ourselves and appreciate ourselves for who we are.

The Infancy Stage

John Vickers was only eight years old when he was brought into a psychiatric clinic for treatment of severe behavior problems. The psychiatric report described him in such terms as "unable to make friends," "detached," "prone to violent temper tantrums," and "unconcerned with rules and regulations."

These descriptions are frequently found in the records of children from unloving, rejecting families. But John came from an apparently loving, stable home background. Why did he show the sort of suspiciousness, hostility, and detachment almost always associated with a lack of loving relationships?

The answer came from an analysis of John's medical history. During his first two years, John had an almost continuous case of skin blisters and rashes. Not only did this make his life miserable, but it also prevented his mother from touching and caressing him. Deprived of this most basic form of love, John grew up unable to love others.

The infancy period has been called the "stage of trust versus mistrust." If a child has a secure, stimulating relationship with his mother or a consistent mother-figure, he will grow up with a healthy, trusting attitude toward the world. On the other hand, if his early contact is impersonal, cold, and indifferent, he will grow up like John Vickers. His conscience will be weak and his love shallow.

About fourteen years ago one of my friends adopted a three-year-old girl. He and his wife are a lovely Christian couple—dedicated, Spirit-filled people with high ideals. But they have been unable to make up for the deficiencies in this girl's early life. Her biological mother, an alcoholic, didn't interact with her. The child received no touching or caressing and only the necessary nutritional provisions. As a result, she has grown up without a conscience—defiant, promiscuous, and unable to learn rules and regulations. She's caused her adoptive parents much grief and heartache.

These two examples illustrate the tremendous impact the infancy stage has upon a person's character and personality. Thankfully, most of us are blessed with parents who recognized and fulfilled their responsibilities.

Psychologists used to believe that children enter the world as "empty tablets" and that parents determine every trait and characteristic of the newborn child. But some exciting new research indicates that children enter the world with their own personality predispositions and that, as often as not, parents react to these existing traits.

Penny's first baby, Robin, was a high-strung little girl who arched her back and stiffened like a board when Penny tried to cuddle her. The only time she'd lie relatively quiet and allow herself to be rocked was while she was nursing. Her mother constantly tried to find ways of physically expressing her love to her tense, nervous daughter.

On the other hand, Penny's second child, Brandon, was a bundle of love from birth. Soft and cuddly, she'd snuggle against her mother long after she'd finished nursing. No less active than Robin, Brandon would stop playing now and then and go to her mother for a few moments of holding and hugging.

And yet, as both girls have grown, Robin has developed qualities of loving sensitivity that her younger sister still lacks. It's not easy to raise a "difficult" baby, but rewards abound for parents who maintain patience.

Psychologists have long known that parents who physically abuse their own children are usually people who were abused themselves. And a child with a very difficult temperament is more likely to be abused than a child with a more easygoing temperament.

Several weeks ago, my wife agreed to babysit for a young couple who wanted to go to a marriage enrichment seminar for the weekend. Their baby girl, we found out, had a "difficult" temperament. She cried almost all the time and was unable to sleep for more than a couple of hours at a time, even at night. She would eat only a small amount of food, and then cry again because she was hungry. Holding, rocking, or walking her gave her no comfort, either. And it was not because we were strangers; the problem went deeper than that.

Nothing we tried to do pleased her, and it was one of the most tiring and frustrating weekends we ever spent. I only hope the child's parents will maintain their patience and love.

Such children are very unrewarding to mothers. Undiagnosed medical problems can make the child seem merely bad. In fact, many physiological and psychological problems cannot be discerned by the average physician, and he gives the baby a clean bill of health. Poor baby . . . poor parents.

If parents aren't patient and mature, they can be provoked into rejecting a difficult child, failing to provide him with adequate love during infancy. While this more often happens with boys (who usually have the more difficult temperaments), girls are not immune.

Ask your mother what kind of temperament you displayed as a child and how she reacted to you. It might help you understand yourself better. Sometimes people find that their own temperaments influenced the way they got along with their parents even years later. What Freud said is probably true: "The child is father to the man [or woman]."

The Childhood Stage

Many books have been written about the childhood stage. I couldn't possibly cover all the important topics in just a few pages. But I would like to describe several important factors that affect the development of girls.

The first is the father's importance in a child's development. When I was in school, psychologists believed that the mother's influence in the family was crucial and the father played a relatively minor role. But we've learned a lot since then. We now know that the father plays a very important role in his children's development.

Girls who grow up without father figures (or with detached, ineffective fathers) often go in one of two directions. Some become sexually promiscuous, frantically substituting physical affection for the love they never received from their fathers. Others become extremely shy and withdrawn around men. They often fear the opposite sex and have stormy courtships and strife-filled marriages. Both men and women who grow up in fatherless homes are more likely to divorce their spouses.

This is not meant to frighten mothers who are raising children alone, but the rise in numbers of single-parent homes is very sad. Girls can gain a lot of security and healthy self-esteem through a loving and affectionate relationship with a strong father. One of the most well-adjusted women I know had a very close relationship with her father (and a loving relationship with her mother). This girl's father was a strong authoritative figure, but he wasn't distant or aloof. He took it upon himself to discuss things with his daughter and to let her know she was important to him. And she thrived and grew under his love and guidance.

If you are in the situation of raising a family alone, it is important that you enlist the help of a father-figure for your children—an uncle, a brother, or your father. The important thing is that he has a genuine interest in your son or daughter and relates well to them. Too often, children live only in a woman's world; even those with fathers at home don't see much of them.

A second factor that becomes important during the childhood stage is the child's "sexual identity." This term usually refers to the extent to which a person feels securely masculine or feminine. Actually, men have much greater problems than women in establishing their sexual identity. Many studies indicate that women are much more secure about their femininity than men are about their masculinity.

In part, these differences stem from the parents. Girls almost always have their mothers present to identify with, but sadly, boys often lack effective fathers. If an effective father figure is not present, boys will be unsure about their masculinity.

Jimmy and Mike are throwing a ball back and forth. Then Kathy comes along. Suddenly Jimmy's throws become wild, and Mike leaps into the air to catch them. Then, without even looking at their ten-year-old friend, the boys begin punching each other and rolling on the ground. You've seen it happen lots of times. Little boys ride their bikes faster than ever when little girls come by. And young men feel compelled to "burn rubber" when others are watching.

Women are often irritated by men's desire to "prove themselves." Their need to show off and perform seems strange to women, whose secure sexual identities don't create the sort of insecurity men experience.

Dependency is another outgrowth of a girl's stronger attachment to her mother. Boys usually shift the focus of their identification from their mother to their father, while girls remain firmly identified with their mother. This process of shifting attachment from the mother to the father may help boys become more independent, while the continuing attachment of girls to their mothers may encourage greater dependence.

In this country we place a great value upon independence, often blinding ourselves to the benefits of dependence. Psychoanalysts have long recognized that children's dependence makes it easier for parents to train them. If our children weren't dependent upon us, it would be almost impossible to instill our values in them. Because girls are more dependent upon their parents, I suspect they acquire traits of responsibility, conscientiousness, and morality to a greater extent than boys.

But dependence upon parents has another benefit. Little girls, being more wrapped up with their mothers, receive more affection, nurture, and love, and *by so doing become more affectionate, nurturing, and loving*. These experiences are crucial in preparing girls for their future role as mothers, and for giving them the gentleness and tenderness so integral to the Christian character.

Several years ago, psychologist Beatrice Wright wrote an article entitled "A New Look at Overprotection and Dependency," in which she called into question the traditional negative view of dependency and presented evidence suggesting that some kinds of dependence, if not extreme, could actually be beneficial.[1] She pointed out that none of us are completely independent. We all depend on other people for both love and service. Maturity is, in part, an ability to accept our own dependence.

Handicapped and mentally retarded children are protected and allowed to be dependent much longer than other children. And these are the very children that we so often find to be loving, appreciative, and affectionate.

Soonja, a Korean mother in the United States, amazed her American friends because of the way she taught her babies to be dependent upon her. But Soonja merely laughed at them. "In Korea, the mothers keep their babies tied to their backs, and then the older sisters tote the toddlers about. We keep them with us—really dependent—until they're about five. They're happy and secure, and better able to be independent later.''

To her friends' surprise, that's just what happened with Soonja's boys. Everyone thought they were terribly spoiled and overprotected, but even though one was outgoing and the other shy, by age six they both were happy, well-adjusted, and independent.

The final factor that affects development, in addition to the father figure, sexual identity, and dependency, is the sense of competence. This also is affected by the dependence of the child upon the parents.

Children need a certain amount of freedom to explore their environments. Johnny learns what he can control only by experience. He fills his wagon with dead leaves, and he can pull it easily. He fills it with rocks and boards, and he can hardly budge it. By thrusting outward into the world, children develop a sense of competence and mastery.

This does not mean you push Suzy and Mark out the door in the morning and lock it until dark. The simple act of being responsible for certain tasks—such as keeping dolls and trucks in a specific place—gives children a sense of control over their environment. Every child needs to feel he has some control over his existence, that he can make his will felt upon his surroundings. Parents can allow children to make simple choices. Does Kelly want juice in her orange or blue cup? Does Randy want to wear his red shirt or his yellow one? If we as parents interfere too much with this process, our children may grow up feeling incompetent, with a poor self-concept.

One of the saddest stories I've heard concerns a blind man who received his sight. The story was widely publicized in the London *Daily Telegraph* more than twenty years ago. This man had been blind since ten months of age, the victim of an eye infection. But he had adapted to his disability quite well. He had ridden on motorcycles, walked all over town with just a cane, and had supported himself and his family quite well as a shoe repairman. His competence was amazing, and his self-concept was strong and positive.

At age fifty-two this man received surgery at the Royal Birmingham Eye Hospital in England. Almost immediately after the operation, he could see and recognize common objects around him and engage in most of the activities performed by sighted persons.

But soon it was obvious that he could not function as well as a sighted person as he had as a blind person. For one thing, years of depending upon touch to guide him made it difficult to adjust to vision. He couldn't estimate height very well. He still depended upon voices to recognize people. Overall, he functioned poorly as a sighted person. As a result, soon after his operation he sank into a deep depression. He sat in the dark for hours, listening to the radio. Only a year after the operation he died, the victim of a shattered self-concept.

Both boys and girls need to feel competent in order to develop healthy self-concepts. Usually this is less a factor for boys than it is for girls. The independence, aggressiveness, and energy of little boys just naturally thrust them out into the world and help them acquire a sense of mastery and competence. They climb trees, dig holes, and build forts. But little girls often have to be gently encouraged in their tentative excursions outward, just as little boys need to be encouraged to express love and tenderness, which often come easier to girls.

This doesn't mean we should try to force the same temperament on boys and girls equally. In the first place, that would be impossible, given their different natures. Second, it would be undesirable. It would violate the law of complementarity, which says that marriage and sexual relationships are strengthened when each partner contributes something the other cannot as easily provide. In this way, men and women need one another more than they would if both were independent, self-sufficient beings.

Girls should be encouraged in their attempts to master their environments, but they should not be pressured to compete with boys. Your daughters will express their interests to you. Elizabeth has had a love affair with rocks and minerals ever since she could hold them in her hand. At age twelve, she finds and recognizes fossils and rocks and checks out library books to identify them. Although she willingly performs some domestic jobs for her family, her love is elsewhere.

Her little brother Tommy has all the domestic qualities she lacks. He enjoys cooking and doesn't mind cleaning up afterwards. Yet he also has an obvious bent toward "boy" activities. He has an analytical mind and wants to know how everything works. But their parents have not pressured either child to excel in areas where they have no interest, for that would lead to lowered self-esteem.

Today's trend is for everyone to value and develop "masculine" attributes—aggressiveness, competitiveness, and dominance. We even demand this of our daughters. But unless we begin to give equal importance to the "feminine" traits of gentleness, affection, and nurture, we might find ourselves living in a ruthlessly competitive and cruel world. The core of the masculine/feminine relationship is that both roles are indispensable.

The Adolescent Stage

During a class on psychological testing, a young graduate student asked his professor the following question: "What would you say about a person who seems well-adjusted and healthy, but his test results indicate a lot of pathology, low self-esteem, and poor social relationships?"

His professor quickly replied: "I'd say that either he's an expert at hiding his true nature, or else he's an adolescent."

Adolescence is a stormy, stressful, painful period. In fact, psychologists are encouraged to observe the following rule when interpreting the personality tests of young people: What would be considered pathological (abnormal) at other ages is often very normal at adolescence.

Because their sexual and aggressive drives are stronger, boys possibly experience greater feelings of instability than girls do at puberty. But neither sex is immune. For girls, the beginning of menstruation produces both positive and negative changes that boys never experience. Recent research shows that during the time girls begin to menstruate, they have the same hormones surging through their bodies as do pregnant women. Is it any wonder their moods are so extreme!

Puberty usually begins around age eleven for girls, almost two years before it commences in boys. As a result, girls undergo the "growth spurt" earlier—a process that soon turns their romantic interests away from boys their own age toward boys a little older. The "breast bud" is one of the first signs that a girl is becoming a woman. Soon afterward, estrogen, the female hormone, floods her body and causes her sexual organs—the uterus, labia, clitoris, and vagina—to enlarge. Immediately after that, her bones begin to expand. The pelvis widens, so that children may be born.

Of course, the most obvious indicator that a young girl has reached puberty is her first menstrual period. Several factors influence how a girl feels about this sign of womanhood: how well her mother prepared her for it, her attitude toward growing up, and the behavior of other girls.

When Jimi began menstruation, she was scared to death. Because she was only ten, her mother had not told her about it yet. So Jimi took great care to share this part of growing up with her oldest daughter when she was only nine. As it happened, when this daughter had her first period at ten and a half, Jimi's eight-year-old daughter demanded to know what was going on. The younger girl began to menstruate two months later, a week short of her ninth birthday.

The menstrual period provides girls with something boys don't have—a definite sign of sexual maturity and identity. The male body has no similar index of manhood. This probably adds to his problem of achieving sexual identity. Many cultures have "rites of passage"—ceremonies designed to tell young people that "you are no longer a child; you are now an adult." These ceremonies almost always involve the boys, rarely the girls. Often the boys must go out and kill a certain wild animal, or spend a few days alone in the wild. In some cultures, the rites involve cutting around the genitals. It's as if the culture is trying to provide boys with a definite sign of sexual maturity and identity.

One factor that influences a girl's attitude toward menstruation is the experience of her age-mates. We all tend to compare ourselves with others, and this tendency is even stronger at puberty. Actress Liv Ullmann, in her book *Changing,* describes her own experience as a "late maturer."

> Most girls missed once a month by saying "usual reason" in a matter-of-fact voice when their names were called out. And when it never happened to me, I pretended it had, but I could never keep track of the dates. For a whole year I was a fraud—without realizing that all the others knew, only the teacher had asked them to be tactful and pretend they didn't.[2]

The horror of being behind the others in important signs of maturity can obviously leave long-lasting impressions. Generally, boys are hurt by late puberty more than girls are. We can all sympathize with boys who lag several inches behind the girls in height. But no girl can imagine the agony of the boy who's still four-foot-eleven or five-foot-one, when his age-mates are stretching toward six feet. Eighth-grade Alex hung by his legs from the swing bar every afternoon, then ran into the house to measure himself. It didn't work, and until Alex began a growth spurt at sixteen, he suffered the torments of the damned.

But "tardy" adolescent girls are not immune. "You don't know what it's like," Barbie sobbed, "to have to undress in gym class and not even *need* a bra." Late menstruation can have a profound impact on someone who's already undergoing an identity crisis. Little insults and embarrassments can have a cumulative effect; their impact can be so crushing that future happiness and maturity are hampered.

When you are unable to master the most important tasks

at one stage of development, you will find it more difficult to handle the tasks at future stages. The excruciating pains that occur during adolescence, when an identity is being formed, often result in an uncertain identity—a weak self-concept—even into middle age.

Lisa was an average thirteen-year-old, no prettier or less attractive than the others. But she was shy, and she had unusually dark eyebrows for her fair skin and blonde hair. Jenny—a leader—decided that Lisa had "furry eyebrows." At a time when Lisa especially needed friends, the nickname "furry eyebrows" stuck. Her peers weren't consciously unkind, but they needed friendship with Jenny more than with Lisa.

As an adult, Lisa can look back with a wistful smile at that terrible year. She knows there was no rational reason the girls singled her out for torment, but she still finds it hard to approach anyone new. She's afraid of rejection.

One of the nastiest barriers to a secure sense of identity among young people is that scourge of the shy: the clique. Pecking orders will usually form wherever people get together in groups. But in adolescence, they tend to become more rigid, closed, and hostile to outsiders.

I suppose the natural insecurity of adolescents makes them more prone to form very solid cliques, and more susceptible to the manipulations of someone with a strong will. I say this because I've noticed that the female clique is almost always headed by an attractive (but rarely stunning) girl who knows the latest fashions, is very forward and self-assured, gossips unashamedly, comes from a somewhat snobbish family, and has a great sense of confidence in her ability to manipulate people. She can begin her undisputed leadership in early childhood.

For some strange reason, she also needs to find at least one "whipping girl" a month—that is, a girl to ostracize from the group. Almost all the girls serve as whipping girls at one time or another. The experience, as they report it, is traumatic. It is an unusual girl who, aware of her own inherent value as a child of God, can go through such an experience and retain a healthy self-concept. At the very least, the ostracized girl is hurt for the duration, even though she knows it's not her fault. And many times the hurt goes much deeper.

Some girls never belong to cliques. If they're lucky, it's because they have enough maturity and independence to get along well without them. That type is in the minority, though. Most of the girls who don't join cliques simply lack whatever quality the clique values—money, personality, social standing, and beauty are the usual attributes. Some are simply too shy.

This doesn't have to happen, however. My friend Pauline insists that she didn't grow up that way. "I'm baffled by the way my daughter's friends treat each other," she told me. "I went to a small Christian school and, sure, we had best friends, but they didn't change every time the wind blew. There were several of us who grew up together, and we had a wonderful time. As new girls moved in, we accepted them." Her eyes sparkled. "Some of them didn't accept us. Sue sat during recess reading *The Rise and Fall of the Roman Empire* and turned up her nose at our silliness. Yet later, even she joined us at slumber parties and such." Pauline sighed. "Were we that different from the norm? We didn't realize it."

One of the problems with the power of adolescent cliques is that the fears and preoccupations it encourages may go with the person throughout life. Take popularity, for example. A woman told me that even at middle age she had strong insecurities over her popularity. She worried often whether the other women at church liked her, and she dreaded inviting another couple to dinner for fear they wouldn't accept her. Actually, she had never learned to accept herself.

Other people try to form cliques even in middle age. People who do this were usually part of the "in crowd." When I first began teaching college, I struck up a friendship with another professor just a few years older than I. He had grown up in a wealthy family and was accustomed to the status and prerogatives it brought. He and his wife had formed a clique with several other couples, and they tried to pull my wife and me into it. We resisted, and quickly incurred the group's disapproval. Presently the clique fell apart, as several of the couples divorced or moved away. My friend and his wife went through a period of mourning, until they were able to form another clique with two other couples.

The woman who headed the adolescent girls' clique almost always marries a well-to-do man and carries on a fairly successful life of social advancement. The skills she learned in the adolescent clique serve her well in a materialistic, snobbish social circle. But they don't help her character. That's the worst result. Her success at manipulation encourages traits of egotism and arrogance that make it hard for her to develop humility and a love of service, even if she is a Christian.

For this reason, it's imperative that we outgrow the adolescent orientation. Concern with popularity, obsession with status within a peer group, social competitiveness, and preoccupation with self all must be overcome if we are to grow up toward Christian maturity. For those of us who have problems in this area, that's easier said than done. I believe that Christian women don't feel a need for popularity nearly as much if they have fully accepted—and learned to be happy with—themselves.

Noelle is slim, five-feet-ten, and has pale blond hair. She is an attractive woman and is happy with herself. But if she had less maturity, she could brood about her looks. She never developed the soft, rounded figure she wanted, and her hair will not hold a set. When she puts on three-inch heels she's six-feet-one. Any of these minor problems could destroy a woman who has a poor self-image in the first place. You might have noticed that American advertising encourages women to be unhappy with what they are— whatever they are! And since today's trend is toward the preoccupations of adolescence, more and more people are acting like adolescents. Youth worship and the dread of old age is one example of this immaturity.

The Intimacy Stage

Around the age of twenty or so, the mature person starts to move away from adolescent preoccupations in the process of confronting adult responsibilities and tasks. I don't think it's accurate to say that if you failed at any of the previous stages, you will automatically fail at future stages. I've known some people with painful childhoods and unsuccessful adolescent periods who still went on to gain maturity in adulthood. And yet, the experiences we had at earlier stages definitely influence our ability to handle the requirements of subsequent stages.

Entire books have been written on the subject of maturity—what it is and how to achieve it. I couldn't possibly cover many aspects of the issue in a few short paragraphs. But in part, maturity involves leaving behind the preoccupations associated with the previous stages. And Christian maturity involves much more than that, for it is spiritual as well as emotional.

As a woman leaves adolescence, the maturity she achieves should involve a gradual shedding of the preoccupations with identity and the peer group, in favor of confronting the new tasks of intimacy with another person and preparing for adult responsibilities. This is a gradual process of maturity; no one achieves it quickly.

One of the major tasks a person faces in his early-to-mid twenties is establishing an intimate relationship with a member of the opposite sex—in other words, setting up a family. The word "intimacy" does not refer only to sexual relationships. It means the ability to share with and care about another person without fear of losing oneself in the process. This ability is a highly important prerequisite for the establishment of long-lasting, satisfying marriages. With so many marriages ending in divorce, let's look at the important elements in successful, intimate marriages.

Patricia O'Brien wrote an interesting article entitled "How to Survive the Early Years of Marriage."[3] In it she reports the results of a survey she undertook to answer the

question, "What makes a successful marriage?" She identified four necessary ingredients.

The first is a *realistic, productive courtship*. The engage-
ment period is not just a time of waiting for marriage; it is a
time for preparation for marriage. It is a time to learn to
know each other's personality and basic philosophy, to
make sure you and your prospective mate are truly compatible. It is a time to shed illusions about "living happily
ever after."

Jerry and Charlotte came from two different worlds . . .
and met in college and married. But before they tied the
knot, they explored their differences and the adjustments
they knew were inevitable. Although they were both
Christians, they had more marital problems than the average couple. Yet they never stopped being tolerant of one
another, and they continued to grow together. They were
proud of each other, filling their days with as many expres-
sions of love and affection as possible. After many years,
this unlikely marriage is still strong and rewarding.

Rabbi Edwin Friedman, a family therapist at Georgetown
University Medical School, claims that ". . . young couples who are the most romantic in planning their weddings
are the ones most likely to break up early."

I remember when Rhonda and Kent were married. Eigh-
teen-year-old Rhonda planned a magnificent wedding.
Kent's father gave them a "honeymoon cottage," and the
two dreamed of waking each other up with kisses by morning and falling asleep in each other's arms at night. These
are lovely sentiments, but they don't have much to do with
the reality of daily living.

After a year of marriage, Kent, still in college, noticed
that some of the co-eds weren't as demanding as Rhonda.
Kelly especially delighted in his witticisms. Kent saw
Rhonda when she was tired, when she grew impatient with
his sloppiness, when she resented his staying out late. Kelly
looked better to him than Rhonda, so he left her for Kelly.

Marriage is not like living in a fairy tale, and people who
shed that illusion the earliest are the least likely to be rudely
shocked in the first few months. Marriage is a growing

process, and true growth almost always involves some pain. Marriage is also adjusting to another person's weaknesses and desires. It involves both deep rewards *and* nagging demands. We shouldn't overlook either.

The second factor in successful early years of marriage is *the image problem*. During courtship, we easily see our future mate's strengths, rarely observing the weaknesses. But those quickly become apparent after marriage.

Trudy admired her husband's self-confidence and sense of mastery. But when he lost his job six months after they were married, some of his insecurities and self-doubts surfaced. "I'm no good. You never should have married me," he whimpered. He felt too depressed to look for work. She tried to be supportive, but she was just too scared and shocked. It took several months of mutual patience and support before he got a new job and returned to his old self.

Often, a young couple will find they cannot rely only on one another but must depend on relatives as well. Annie and Jim's first apartment was furnished with surplus from her parents' home, and Meg's parents offered to continue to pay her college tuition when she married a year before graduation. I see nothing undesirable about this, as long as it's not carried to an extreme. Families are meant to be supportive. The demand to "do it ourselves" is an extreme reaction to unresolved adolescent anxieties. Family members—aunts, uncles, fathers, mothers, brothers, sisters— are a great resource. They can often see a young couple through rough times, emotionally as well as financially.

The third factor is *children*. Many couples are settling the issue by not having children, but I don't think that is God's plan. Perhaps it depends on their reason for remaining childless. Lois put her hands on her hips and strutted before her confused mother-in-law. "I'm not going to ruin *my* figure by having brats! Ted and I aren't going to be tied down to any snot-nosed kid. We need our freedom." And truly, it would be a tragedy for Lois to inflict her resentment on an innocent child.

Many couples are putting off childbearing until they are well established financially. Andrea and John were both students who wisely put off having a family. Besides, they weren't sure children would fit into their lifestyle. Several years passed, and they became established in their occupations. "Our lives were full," Andrea said, and John added, "But not full enough." So they started a family, and Andrea restricted her work to one day a week while the children were growing up.

I don't believe a couple should try to have children in their first year or two of marriage. Generally, a two- or three-year adjustment period is needed. Frequently an even longer period is beneficial. My wife and I waited more than seven years to have children. I've never regretted the decision, for we both needed that valuable growing-up period.

The fourth factor is *money*. For the couple contemplating marriage, sex is a much more interesting topic. But the fact is that money worries cause a lot more marital problems than lovemaking does. When the fun is over, the unpaid bills are still waiting. Years ago, the bride's family handled this issue by requiring young men to show evidence that they could provide for a family before they would allow their daughters to marry. Today, most young people are free to do as they please after they are eighteen. Many Christian colleges try to discourage marriage before graduation. And in most marriages, both partners work for at least a few years after marriage.

The factors that affect this "stage of intimacy" require much attention, for they will affect a woman's self-esteem for years to come. The failure to establish a strong marriage probably has a more negative effect on adult self-esteem than any other single factor.

The Productivity Stage

As young people move into their middle twenties and early thirties, they enter the most productive period of their lives. Children are born and reared, and productive skills are developed during this period. In a sense, this could be called the "age of creativity."

A woman's satisfaction with the role of motherhood depends in large part upon what's happened in the earlier stages. Was she loved and secure during her earliest years and beyond? Was she allowed and encouraged to develop a feeling of competence, so that now she can assert herself in a healthy way with her own children? Does she have a clear sense of who she is, and enough independence from the peer group to live her own life? Has she been able to establish a stable, intimate relationship with her husband? These are the factors that will affect her during this stage of development.

Having children brings about changes in our lives; there's no doubt about that. Some research suggests that marital intimacy and satisfaction suffer during the years children are being reared, and when children finally leave home, the parents don't even know each other. Of course, there are many rewards as well.

But it's important to emphasize that husbands and wives have to work at intimacy. It came more easily and naturally in the previous stage; now it requires more effort. Time must be set aside for the couple to be alone together and talk. Whether this happens once a day or once a week, it is vital to a successful relationship. How well this is managed, and how persistently husbands and wives are willing to pursue it, affects the marital satisfaction of many couples.

Like so many couples, Gina and Phil fell into a trap. As a minister, Phil spent his days and evenings taking care of the needs of his church members. Gina stayed home with their three stair-step children.

Some women have a way of suppressing frustration and anger, hoping it will go away. Gina began to resent her husband's board meetings and the problem-filled church members, and she became angry that she didn't get to see more of Phil.

She simmered, throwing out hints of her anger. But Phil didn't notice. Oh yes, he commented that she was impatient with the children and teased her because she let his dinner burn when he was late. But he was too busy and too easygoing to be aware that their marriage was in trouble.

This is the point where wives often pick up and move out. But not Gina. In fact, she was so immersed in her first love—homemaking/mothering—that she only tried harder. She spent more time with the children, fixed even better dinners, and kept the house even cleaner. Of course, that was not the solution.

Gina exploded.

All the hurt and loneliness she'd kept inside came pouring out. Phil couldn't understand; he had thought they were happy. Fortunately for both of them, Phil sensed Gina's plea for love and attention, and the two sat down to make changes. They budgeted time to be alone and time for Phil to spend with the kids. Phil wrote "Family" in his appointment book and refused other engagements during those times. It didn't happen overnight, but today Gina and Phil have a good marriage.

Another factor that can increase a woman's satisfaction is the feeling that her work is worthwhile and lasting. For the full-time homemaker and mother, this feeling may be hard to achieve, especially if she listens to popular messages and slogans. Husbands can help their wives' adjustment to their never-ending job by taking their share of the responsibility for the children. Psychological research has refuted the idea that all a father needs to do is provide for his family. Not only do children need regular contact with their fathers, but mothers need to be relieved of their duty from time to time. Happy is the wife whose husband is willing to take time with his children.

Women at this stage often feel a need to produce something that is not immediately used up, eaten, or messed up. One young mother told me, "I sometimes feel that almost everything I do is quickly erased. I devote hours to preparing a meal, and it's eaten in thirty minutes. I wash clothes, and they're dirtied. That's why I wrote a book. Even if it's never published, at least it was something that couldn't be immediately erased." I suspect that this desire to produce something that isn't temporary is a major impetus behind women's love of sewing. The product lasts for years instead of minutes. And the activity can be therapeutic.

One of the major challenges a woman faces during this stage, especially if she has been a full-time homemaker, is the "empty nest syndrome." This occurs when all the children are either in school full-time or have left home. Much of the work she used to do has been eliminated. If handled positively, this can be a very creative time of life. Frances took LPN training after she retired. She'd worked in a factory until age sixty, but she had always wanted to be a nurse. She's never been happier. During this stage, a wife can return to work with no major disruption in family life; she can devote more time to church work, go back to school, or do volunteer work. The possibilities are numerous.

The final hurdle that confronts women during this stage is the process of aging and menopause. As was true of the menstrual cycle, menopause has emotional side effects. It is a purely physiological process; the ovaries run out of eggs and periods become irregular, eventually stopping altogether. The decrease in estrogen production causes the symptoms usually referred to as the "change of life." The mood changes involved in this process have been the source of many jokes, but the experience is not humorous to someone going through it.

Aging is another problem for some women. I knew a woman who dreaded it so much that she told her friends nothing could be worse. One night while driving home, she had a head-on collison with another car and neutralized her worst fear. She left behind three children. As the old saying goes, "Getting old is no fun; but when you consider the alternative. . . ."

Aging and menopause are inevitable. Mature women accept the process of growing old and turn their attention to other things. I suspect that those who have lived full, productive lives, and have been able to keep an abiding joy based on their relationship with God, are better able to confront the aging process—and even enjoy it—than those who haven't.

The Retirement Stage

According to some stage theorists, the final stage is one of looking backward, reflecting upon all that's happened in the previous stages. According to this view, happiness at the last stage of life depends more upon what's happened in the earlier stages than it does upon successful mastery of new tasks.

To a certain extent, this may be true. But I think the retirement years can be a time of new challenges also.

Upon retirement, James joined an organization of volunteer workers who travel about the United States (and the world) building schools, churches, clinics, and homes in areas where financial resources are insufficient. "I'm not a carpenter," he says cheerfully, "but they need someone to fetch and carry."

Retirement can also be a time of looking toward the future. One ninety-two-year-old man bought a large piece of land. When asked what he planned to do with it, he replied, "Well, I think I'll let it sit for a few years; then I'll develop it."

Happy are those who refuse to give in to inactivity during the last stage of life. Some women find it a time to do all the handwork—crocheting, quilting, needlepoint, and so forth—that they never had time for when they were younger. Many boutiques stock and sell handwork at a handsome profit.

Other women, especially those whose families are far away, find joy in volunteer work at children's hospitals. "Grandmothers" for handicapped children is another idea that benefits both the woman and the child. A few hours a week of love and attention by an "adopted grandmother" gives these children—whose familes are often absent—a whole new outlook on life.

Anne's grandmother found great satisfaction in teaching Anne the details of fine sewing. In the last year of her life, the two made Christmas tablecloths involving fine handwork, reupholstered and painted a dining room suite, and hand-quilted a Dutch doll quilt that Grandmother had begun forty years before.

Still other women write the family history, including details of the "olden days."

"I know there's probably not a soul alive who gives a rip that we cleaned our kerosene lamp chimneys with newspapers, but I'm writing it down anyway. And milking that mean old cow who slapped me in the face with her manure-caked tail." She laughs. "Life today is so different. Someday one of my grandkids will be interested."

For many Christians, the last stage is a time for Bible study and intercessory prayer. I know one woman who devoted much of her time to praying for her children and relatives. Although she wasn't as physically active as she had been in the past, her will still reached out in unselfish service to others.

Miss Mary had a faraway look in her eyes, and I asked her, "Where are your thoughts?" She smiled. "You'd never guess. In Tokyo. I have been praying for our church members in that city." Her cheerful letters have brought encouragement to people all over the world. "I have chosen you as my prayer project for the first week in April," she might write to a missionary in Libya or a school teacher in New York. "Don't feel that you must reply. Just know that I am praying for you in a special way."

To a large extent, this last stage of life is one in which the family once again becomes as important as it was during the first stage. Older people who enjoy this stage the most almost always seem to be those who can turn to their "children's children" for satisfaction, basking in the warm glow of the close-knit, loving family relationships they cultivated during their adult lives.

Unmarried women enjoy nieces and nephews and children of friends. Perhaps it doesn't matter so much *whose* family it is, as long as they are able to maintain a close relationship with someone. In today's mobile society, some young families have advertised for "grandparents"—someone to share all the little joys that make up their everyday lives.

This confirms all the studies that show that the family, above all other earthly institutions, is the main source of individual happiness and satisfaction.

Ten

What to Do About Low Self-Esteem

I know a woman who has every "right" to have low self-esteem. When Jan was only five years old, her family was disrupted by her father's death. Her mother was a very critical and insecure woman who frequently ridiculed her daughter. Jan married a man with the same weaknesses, and he spent the next twenty-five years making sure she had a good grasp of her own shortcomings and failings. He lost a good job a few years before he died, forcing her to seek work while in her fifties. Shortly after her husband died, she lost her only son in a car accident.

These experiences would devastate most of us. But Jan seems unshaken. Her sense of self—her acceptance of who she is—remains as strong as ever. She is kind, loving, patient, and giving. Low self-esteem is not a problem. She seems able to forget about herself, losing herself in service to others.

It would be nice if we could shake off defeats and circumstances so easily, but most of us lack the self-protective device this woman possessed.

We all want to protect our self-esteem, even if we're not concerned with raising it. Each of us has an optimal level of self-esteem, and we want to avoid threats to that optimal level.

I believe there are more threats to women's self-esteem than there are to men's. If we could change *men,* and strengthen the *family*, we'd go a long way toward removing many of those threats. But since an ideal social situation will not occur until Christ returns, we need resources to help us deal with the problems of self-esteem.

No perfect solution exists, despite the promises of many popular books. But all of us have the capacity to grow, if we're nurtured properly. Here are some suggestions for the woman who needs a lift in self-esteem.

1. *Don't compare yourself with others.* The tendency to do this is so strong that it must be resisted constantly. There's no better way to make yourself feel gloomy, worthless, and pessimistic than to become obsessed with someone who has more money, a more pleasing personality, higher status . . . and on and on.

All gifts come from God. Each of us has some talents, even though they may be undeveloped. Our goal should be to develop the gifts we do possess and not to worry about people who have more than we do. When Dana complimented Jenny on her smile, Jenny laughed. "I'm so glad you said that! I prayed for this smile for two years. I know I'm plain and I was so shy, but I prayed and prayed that God would give me a smile so I could at least *look* friendly."

2. *Accept your basic personality style and work from there.* For many people, the past two decades have been a time of searching for identity. Traditional roles, which gave us so much guidance and support, are no longer clearly defined. Many people move from one place to another every few years, so that a feeling of rootedness and belonging is hard to maintain. People leave their extended families—usually a source of stability—to live in places far away.

When Marguerite moved to a small town, she carried a trunkful of dreams. Married three years and living a thousand miles from her family, she'd been lonely in their city apartment. But moving to a little community seemed like the answer. Marguerite pictured herself sitting on a blanket and talking with the neighbors while their babies romped in the grass. In reality, the neighbors were so involved with their extended families that they hardly knew the newcomers were there!

This rootlessness of modern industrial living has tended to favor some personality styles more than others. Several recent books point out that the type of personality that gets along best today is quite different from the one that thrived in the past. The new "healthy" man (or woman) is flexible, outgoing, adaptive, and liberated from traditional restraints. Since he will probably move several times throughout his life, he must be able to adapt to new values and styles of living. He must be able to shed old values in order to adopt the standards of new (and different) peer groups. He must be, in other words, a chameleon, able to change colors at will.

But this new man or woman is to a large extent incompatible with Christianity. Our values and goals are unchangeable and timeless. We cannot shed them when they become inconvenient. Neither can we afford to develop shallow, fleeting friendships at the expense of deeper family relationships. Nor can we allow others to train our children because childrearing ties us down and interferes with our freedom.

Obviously, Christian values are often incompatible with the normless "new humanity." But what's less obvious is that the same conditions that have encouraged the development of the new humanity have also dictated our conception of what an ideal personality looks like. Psychologists, themselves heavily influenced by cultural pressures, too often hold up this conception as if it were an absolute ideal.

We read in popular psychology books that one should be spontaneous rather than restrained. You should "live for the moment"; don't be "tied down by the past"; "be completely independent." This advice champions one personality style as the ideal, failing to recognize or acknowledge the strengths of other personality types.

In a similar manner, our culture has so promoted masculine ideals and attributes that we've failed to appreciate and encourage the feminine ones. Some women viciously deny their own femininity in their quest for masculine goals.

We Christians easily recognize the need to look beyond cultural values toward important absolute moral standards. But less obvious is the need to overcome culture-based personality ideals. Remember that God appreciates your femininity and all that it entails, even if the world doesn't. And He's the only One who really counts.

3. *As much as possible, keep your attention off yourself.* Both physical and emotional pain can engender a curious self-perpetuating cycle. If you bruise your hand, for example, the pain makes you focus attention upon the sore spot. You nurture it, protect it, and think about it. But concentrating on sore spots can increase the discomfort; sometimes healing best takes place when you forget about the sore area.

Low self-esteem can produce a similar pattern. The person with emotional pain is often tempted to become absorbed in his own needs and feelings. He becomes so wrapped up in himself that he can't meet obligations and responsibilities or attend to the needs of others. And so he runs the risk of worsening his pain and unhappiness.

Psychologists have discovered a pattern that is commonly reported among vibrant, healthy people. When asked to describe the time they felt most competent and contented, these people frequently described some activity they were involved in. During this activity, they suddenly experienced a feeling of losing themselves in what they were doing, of practically merging with the activity so that self-consciousness was forgotten. No matter what the activity involved—working with their hands or their minds—they reported doing their most effective work, and feeling most at peace with the world and themselves, during this period when self was forgotten.

When Francine lost her husband, grief threatened to consume her. She didn't need money, and she was too old to get a job, anyway. Friends provided comfort at first, but then they began to withdraw. Francine drew her loneliness around her and shut everybody out. Her only consolation was her daily visit to the cemetery.

But Kathryn, her close friend, wouldn't give up, even though Francine rejected her efforts to draw her out. Finally Kathryn convinced her to come to the hospital where she was a nurse and spend an hour a day in the children's ward.

"I don't even like children," Francine protested. "I've never even had contact with my grandchildren."

She didn't enjoy the first day at the hospital. She felt stiff and uncomfortable when the little patients clutched at her or called her over to their beds. The next day didn't go much better. She read a story to a little boy in a body cast whose family lived miles away, and she rocked a weeping little girl until the child fell asleep. It wasn't until she stopped at the cemetery on her way home that she realized she hadn't thought about her husband while she rocked and sang to the little girl.

The kids were waiting for her the next day with smiles and calls to "come to my bed . . . come help me." It upset her a little, to be needed. She almost felt panicky, but the feeling left as she forgot herself while working with the children.

In giving herself to those who needed her, Francine became a new person. It didn't happen in a week or even a month, but gradually she came to terms with the loss of her husband. Only when she reluctantly reached out to help others did her healing begin.

4. *Find a comfortable balance between withdrawal and overeagerness.* When self-esteem is low, there is a tendency to act in one of two ways. Some people withdraw as much as possible from the outside world. They tuck their feelings inside and remove themselves from the presence of others. Alex reacted to pressure that way. Retreating was the only way he could cope. And people left him alone. "Never mind calling Alex. He won't go."

Other people move toward the opposite extreme. They thrust themselves at other people, lapping up every tidbit of attention like a thirsty man at an oasis. They come on too strong, and people back away from them.

Neither strategy is effective. The withdrawn person not only misses out on some of the more enjoyable parts of living, but he also runs the risk of mental deterioration. In the absence of contact with others, he may begin thinking bizarre, suspicious thoughts. Other people can serve as an effective check upon this tendency, but the withdrawn person misses out on this most important resource.

People who react to low self-esteem by becoming over-eager and effusive actually drive others away. One woman said, "Whenever I talk to people, I am so eager to say the right thing that I guess I throw myself at them. Even when I see them fidgeting and looking around, I can't seem to force myself to shut up."

This kind of overeagerness should be actively resisted; it frightens and irritates people. Their rejection makes the overeager person feel more anxious, thus strengthening his desire to please others. It usually takes constant attention and watchfulness to break this pattern.

5. *Know that God loves you.* God's love for humanity is personal and specific. Even if you had been the only sinner, He still would have sent His son to die for you. His love is an energizing power—sustaining us, covering up our weaknesses, taking the edge off our deformities. His love and strength can conquer all our liabilities. If you realize your value as a child of God, you know that it doesn't matter what others do or say to you.

One mother I know impresses her children with their value to her in this way. "If someone had a whole roomful of gold and diamonds and money, and they said to me, 'I'll trade you all this for your little girl,' what do you think I'd say?"

Her child looks up, wondering, her eyes big. "Is that worth hundreds of dollars?"

"Oh yes. Hundreds and hundreds and hundreds of dollars."

"What would you say?" asks Small Daughter.

Her mother grabs her and hugs her. "I'd say, 'Never! Never! Never!' I wouldn't give up my little girl for all the gold and diamonds in the whole world."

And that's how God feels about us, too. Sometimes it's helpful to record answers to prayers or other ways you know God has led you. Then when things get rough, you can look at your list and have a black-and-white account of how He's cared for you. You'll have confidence to ask for His continued help.

6. *Use low self-esteem to thrust you toward God.* People handle low self-esteem in a variety of ways. Some seek promiscuous sexual adventures; some turn to liquor and drugs; some withdraw from the world.

The best way to handle low self-esteem is to use it to motivate you to develop a deeper relationship with Christ. Sometimes human beings need to experience a sense of worthlessness or pain before they are willing to turn to God. The apostle Paul was kept humble and dependent upon God by some "thorn in the flesh." Scripture doesn't reveal what that thorn was, but it must have been painful because Paul spent much time in prayer asking the Lord to remove it. And Paul was not highly sensitive to pain, judging by the number of beatings he endured! Perhaps this thorn was his greatest asset, if it kept him dependent upon God.

Because human nature is sinful, it sometimes turns God's gifts into curses. Wealth, beauty, knowledge, fame, even high self-esteem are blessings that are often allowed to come between us and God. Of these, I think high self-esteem has probably prevented souls from turning to Christ as much as any of the others.

Few things are more horrible than being so physically deformed and ugly that your own mother abandons you. That is what happened to John Merrick. He inherited a disease that made him twisted and dwarflike in stature, caused hideous bone deformities, and made heavy folds of skin along his head and body. Known as "the elephant man," he appeared in freak shows until his manager abandoned him on the streets of a large city, where people turned away from him in horror.

A sympathetic doctor had given John Merrick his business card a few years before, and John made his way to the London hospital where this doctor worked. There he lived out the rest of his life.

One of the first books he had ever read was the *Book of Common Prayer,* and perhaps in part because he had no one else to turn to, John Merrick accepted Christ as his Savior and lived an effective Christian life until the day he died.

Christ is the healing balm for all our maladies. His love and His grace are sufficient for us. They are able to sustain us through all difficulties. His Spirit is the best antidote for low self-esteem.

In fact, having covered all the various influences upon woman's self-esteem, we come back to Christ. We can't deny the natural forces that influence self-esteem. But neither can we fully understand this abstraction that we call self-esteem unless we relate it to our God. Love is the most important influence upon self-esteem, and all love springs from God's love for us. By identifying ourselves with Him, by calling ourselves His children, we insure our own identities. And by taking in His Spirit, we gradually experience the growth and development of our greatest strengths. Life for the Christian person is a process of continual growth and the constant assurance that we are loved, that we are important to Someone else. Our greatest need is not for self-esteem. It's for a connection to Him. After that, self-esteem will take care of itself.

Notes

Chapter 1

1. Frederick Flach, *Choices: Coping Creatively With Personal Change* (New York: Lippincott, 1977).
2. Frank Barron, *Creative Person and Creative Process* (New York: Holt, Rinehart, and Winston, 1969).
3. Zygmunt Piotrowski, *The Perceptanalytic Executive Scale* (New York: Grune and Stratton, 1968), p. 116.
4. Edward Wells and Gerald Marwell, *Self-Esteem: Its Conceptualization and Measurement* (Beverly Hills: Sage Publications, 1976).

Chapter 2

1. Stanley Coopersmith, *The Antecedents of Self-Esteem* (San Francisco: W. H. Freeman, 1967).
2. Theodore Millon, *Modern Psychopathology* (Philadelphia: W. B. Saunders, 1968).

Chapter 3

1. Richard Hagen, *The Bio-Sexual Factor* (New York: Doubleday, 1979), p. 238.
2. Jim Towns, ed., *Solo Flight* (Wheaton, Ill.: Tyndale, 1980).
3. Maggie Scarf, *Unfinished Business* (New York: Doubleday, 1980).
4. Edith S. Gornberg and Violet Franks, *Gender and Disordered Behavior* (New York: Brunner/Mazel, 1979).
5. Carle Zimmerman, *Family and Civilization* (New York: Harper and Row, 1947).
6. John Money, *Love and Love Sickness* (Baltimore: Johns Hopkins University Press, 1980).
7. George Albee, "The Protestant Ethic, Sex, and Psychotherapy," *American Psychologist* (February, 1977), pp. 150–161.
8. Judith Bardwick, *In Transition* (New York: Holt, Rinehart, and Winston, 1979), p. 35.
9. Phyllis Chesler, *Women and Madness* (New York: Avon, 1973).

Chapter Four

1. Piotrowski, *Perceptanalytic Executive Scale,* p. 116.

2. See, for instance, Wayne Dyer, *Your Erroneous Zones* (New York: Funk and Wagnalls, 1976).

3. Hans Eysenck, *The Biological Basis of Personality* (Springfield, Ill.: Charles C. Thomas, 1967).

4. Ibid.

5. Ibid.

6. F. A. Hampton, "Shyness," *Journal of Neurology and Psychopathology* (1927–1928), pp. 124–131.

7. Quoted by Charlotte K. Beyers, "Don't Worry If You're Shy," *Parade* (January 18, 1976), p. 12.

8. Corinne Hutt, *Males and Females* (New York: Penguin Books, 1973).

Chapter Five

1. Jesse Bernard, *The Future of Marriage* (New York: Thomas Y. Crowell, 1971).

2. George Gilder, *Sexual Suicide* (New York: Quadrangle, 1973).

3. W. Peter Blitchington, *Sex Roles and the Christian Family* (Wheaton, Ill.: Tyndale, 1980).

4. Charles W. Socarides, *Beyond Sexual Freedom* (New York: Quadrangle, 1975), p. 23.

5. Margaret Mead, *Male and Female* (New York: Morrow, 1949), p. 173.

6. Gilder, *Sexual Suicide,* p. 204.

7. "Sweden Today: The Status of Women in Sweden." Report to the United Nations, 1968.

8. Marie Meierhofer, "Depression in 3-Month-Old-Infants," *Medical Tribune,* Vol. 13, No. 14 (March 5, 1972).

9. Herbert Hendin, *Suicide and Scandinavia* (New York: Grune and Stratton, 1964).

10. Betty Friedan, "The Second Stage," *Redbook* (January, 1980), p. 49.

11. Gilder, *Sexual Suicide.* See also Hugh Carter and Paul C. Glick, *Marriage and Divorce* (Cambridge: Harvard University Press, 1970).

12. Natalie Gittelson, "Marriage: What Women Expect and What They Get," *McCall's* (January, 1980).

Chapter Six

1. Robert Winch, *Mate Selection* (New York: Harper and Brothers, 1958).

2. David Klimek, *Beneath Mate Selection and Marriage* (New York: Van Nostrand, 1979).

3. Ronald Fieve, *Moodswing* (New York: Morrow, 1975), p. 102.

4. Ibid., p. 107.

Chapter Seven
 1. Paul Robinson, *The Modernization of Sex* (New York: Harper and Row, 1977).
 2. Lonnie Barbach, *For Yourself: The Fulfillment of Female Sexuality* (New York: Anchor Books, 1976), p. 6.
 3. Hagen, *The Bio-Sexual Factor,* pp. 43–46.
 4. Anthony Pietropinto and J. Simenauer, *Beyond the Male Myth* (New York: New American Library, 1978), p. 170.
 5. Seymour Fisher, *Understanding the Female Orgasm* (New York: Basic Books, 1973), pp. 397–98.
 6. Ibid., p. 399.
 7. Hagen, *The Bio-Sexual Factor,* p. 156.
 8. Rita Bass-Hass, "The Lesbian Dyad," *Journal of Sex Research,* Vol. 4, No. 2 (1968), pp. 108–126.
 9. Hagen, *The Bio-Sexual Factor,* p. 47.
10. Allan Bell and Martin Weinberg, *Homosexualities: A Study of Diversity Among Men to Women* (New York: New York University Press, 1978), pp. 81–103.
11. A. Henshel, "Swinging: A Study of Decision-Making in Marriage," *Changing Women in a Changing Society,* ed. J. Huber (Chicago: The University of Chicago Press, 1978).
12. Shere Hite, *The Hite Report* (New York: Dell, 1977), p. 431.
13. Fisher, *Understanding the Female Orgasm,* p. 195.
14. Robert J. and Amy Levin, "Sexual Pleasure: The Surprising Preference of 100,000 Women," *Redbook,* September, 1978. See also Tim and Beverly LaHaye, *The Act of Marriage* (Grand Rapids, Mich.: Zondervan, 1975).

Chapter Eight
 1. W. Peter Blitchington, *The Energy and Vitality Book* (Wheaton, Ill.: Tyndale, 1981).
 2. Katherine Dalton, *The Premenstrual Syndrome* (Springfield, Ill.: Charles C. Thomas, 1964).
 3. Judith Bardwick, *Psychology of Women* (New York: Harper and Row, 1971), pp. 22–35.
 4. Alexander Thomas and Stella Chess, *Temperament and Behavior Disorders in Children* (New York: New York University Press, 1968).

Chapter Nine
 1. Beatrice Wright, "A New Look at Overprotection and Dependency." In Larry Fass (ed.), *The Emotionally Disturbed Child* (Springfield, Ill.: Charles C. Thomas, 1970).
 2. Liv Ullmann, *Changing* (New York: Knapp, 1977), p. 67.
 3. Patricia O'Brien, "How to Survive the Early Years of Marriage," *Redbook* (August, 1978), p. 142.